Introduction

This book supports students preparing for IB Mathematics: Analysis and
Level exam. Written by experienced practitioner and mathematician, this ~~~~~~
practice papers offers thorough preparation for IB assessment. Each practice paper is in line with the IB syllabus and exam board specifications, and provides a rich and varied practice to meet all requirements of Analysis and Approaches, Standard Level, IB mathematics.

Papers are designed to teach students applicable, reusable and faster solutions to common problems. Each paper utilises problems to target areas of mathematics which students often find more difficult in the exam. Solutions provided have been reviewed by many students to ensure that they are easily understandable while being the fastest and most re-applicable.

The practice papers cover the following five distinct topics:
1. Number and Algebra
2. Functions
3. Geometry and Trigonometry
4. Probability and Statistics
5. Calculus

After completing these practice papers, you should be able to:
1. Formulate optimal solutions quicker to any Analysis and Approaches, Standard Level, IB mathematics question
2. More readily apply previously learnt skills on a question to question basis

Analysis and Approaches, Standard Level, IB mathematics practice papers comprises of 2 books. Books 1 and 2 contain practice papers for Papers 1 and 2 in IB, respectively. Each book contains 4 full practice papers and solutions.

Contents

1	Instructions	1
2	Paper 1	2
3	Paper 2	11
4	Paper 3	22
5	Paper 4	32
6	Paper 1 solutions	43
7	Paper 2 solutions	51
8	Paper 3 solutions	61
9	Paper 4 solutions	70

Instructions

- Time allowed for each paper: 1 hour 30 minutes.
- The maximum mark for each paper is 80 marks.
- You are not permitted access to any calculator for the papers.
- A clean copy of the mathematics: analysis and approaches formula booklet is required for each paper.
- Answer all questions.
- Unless otherwise stated in the question, all numerical answers should be given exactly or correct to three significant figures.
- Full marks are not necessarily awarded for a correct answer with no working. Answers must be supported by working and/or explanations. Where an answer is incorrect, some marks may be given for a correct method, provided this is shown by written working. You are therefore advised to show all working.

Paper 1

Section A – Short questions

1   [Maximum mark: 5]

Here is a triangle. $\sin x = \dfrac{3\sqrt{3}}{8}$

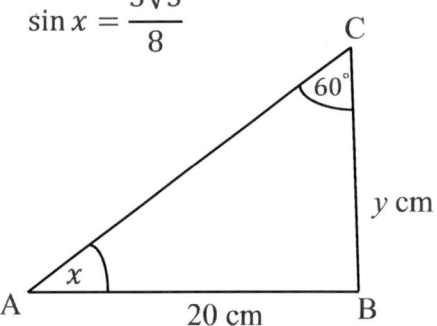

Diagram **NOT** accurately drawn

Work out the value of y.

....

....

....

....

2   [Maximum mark: 5]

ABC is an equilateral triangle. A, B and C are on the circumference of a circle. The length of a side of the equilateral triangle is x cm.

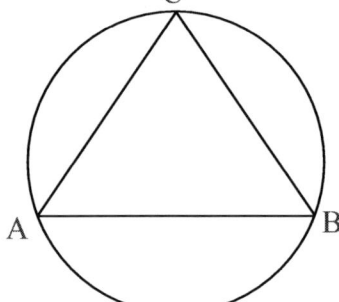

Work out the value of the radius of the circle.

Give your answer in terms of x.

....

....

....

2

3 [Maximum mark: 5]

Consider two consecutive integers, n and $n + 1$.

Prove that the sum of the squares of any two consecutive integers is odd.

....

....

....

....

4 [Maximum mark: 6]

The events A and B are such that $P(A) = 0.3$, $P(B) = 0.5$ and $P(A \cap B) = 0.2$. Find the following probabilities:

(a) $P(A \cup B)$; [3]

....

....

(b) $P(A|B)$. [3]

....

....

5 [Maximum mark: 6]

Let a_n denote the nth term of an arithmetic sequence, and S_n the sum of its first n terms.

(a) Given that $a_3 = 19$ and $S_{25} = 100$, work out the first term and the common difference. [3]

....

....

....

....

....

....

....

(b) Find the least number of terms required for which $S_n < 0$. [3]

....

....

....

....

....

....

....

6   [Maximum mark: 6]

The function f and g are defined such that $f(x) = \dfrac{(x+3)^2}{4}$ and $g(x) = 8x - 2$.

(a) Show that $(g \circ f)(x) = 2(x+2)(x+4)$. [3]

....

....

....

....

....

(b) Given that $(g \circ f)^{-1}(a) = 3$, find the value of a. [3]

....

....

....

....

....

....

7   [Maximum mark: 5]

A curve has equation $y = x^2 + 4x + 4$.

The tangent to the curve at point P on the curve is perpendicular to the line $y = -\frac{1}{2}x + 5$.

Work out the coordinates of P.

Section B – Long questions

8   [Maximum mark: 14]

The sketch shows the curve of $y = f(x)$. The curve passes through the origin O and has a local maximum at $A(1, \frac{2}{3})$ and a local minimum at $B(3, 0)$.

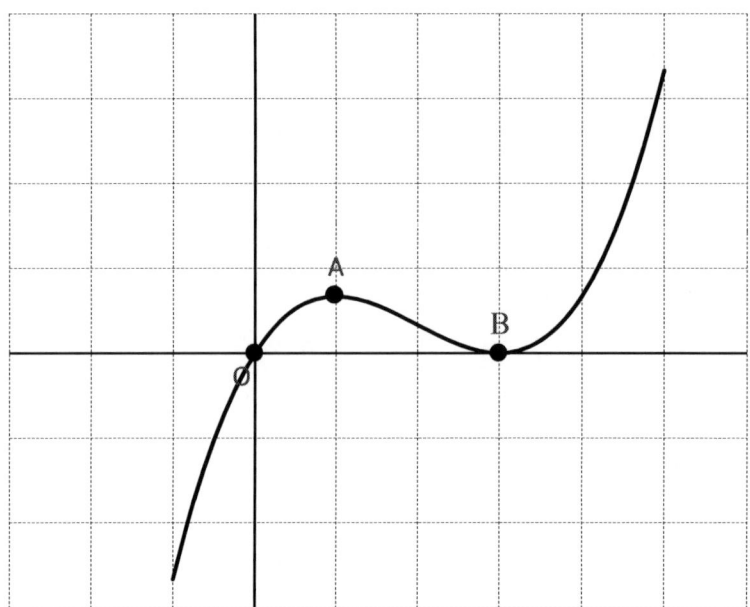

On separate diagrams, sketch the following curves, indicating clearly the coordinates of the images of the points O, A and B.

(a) $y = f(x + 1)$; [3]

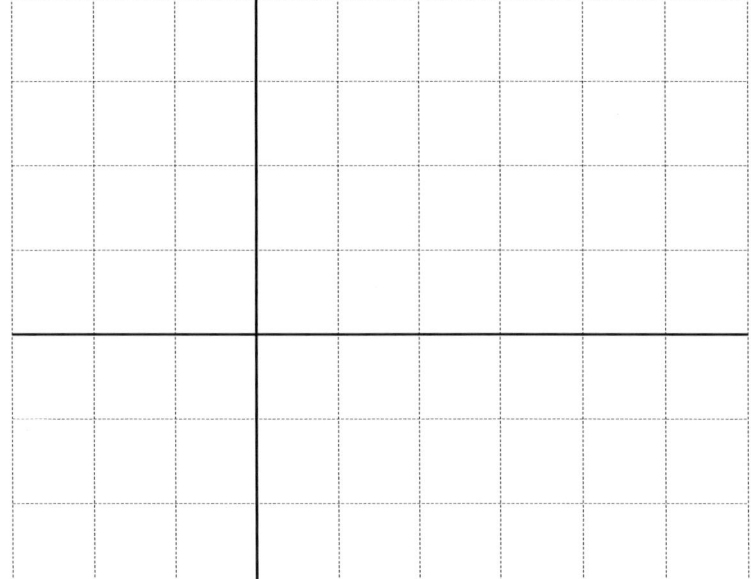

....
....
....
....

(b) $y = 2f(x)$; [3]

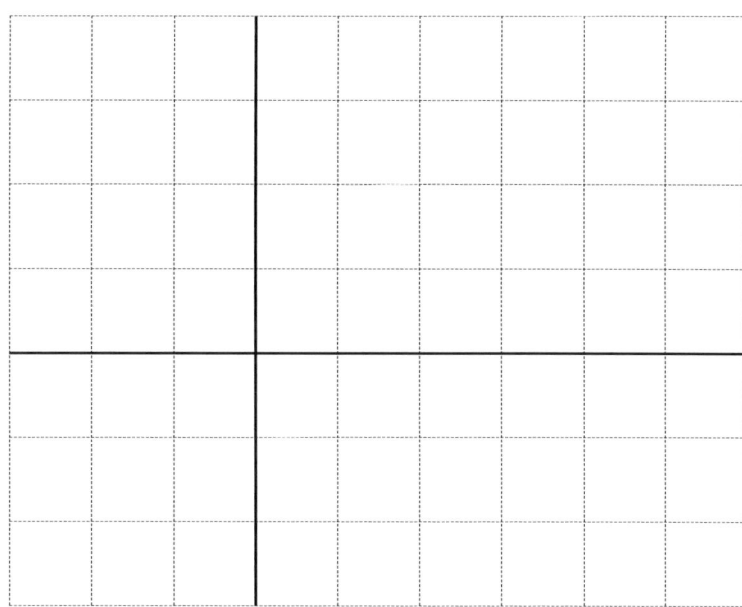

....
....
....

(c) $y = f(2x)$; [3]

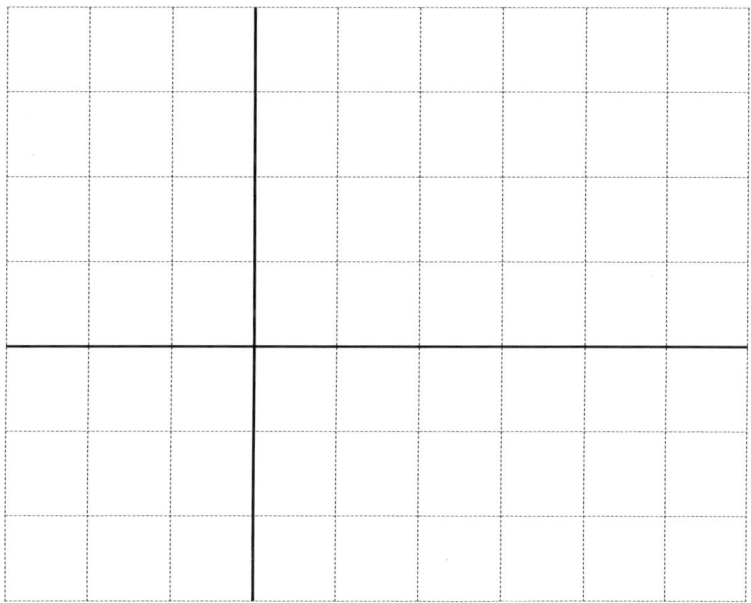

....
....
....

(d) $y = f(2-x)$. [5]

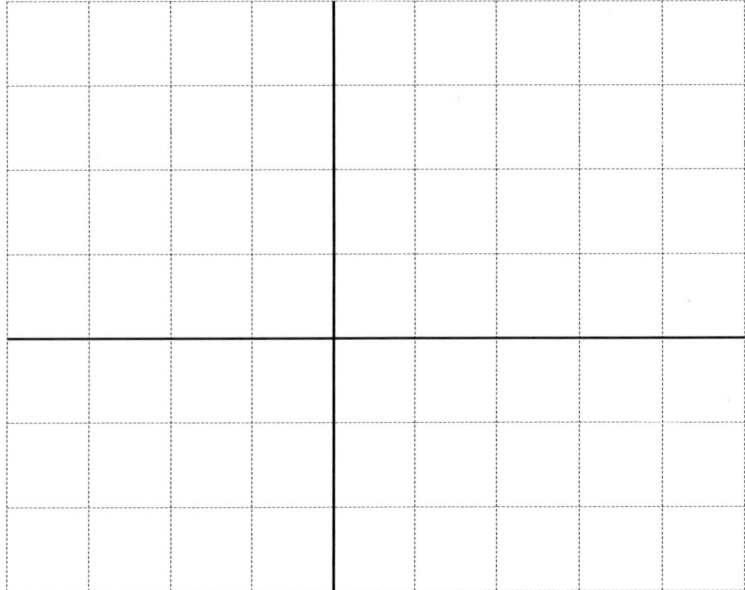

....
....
....

9   [Maximum mark: 16]

The function f is defined for all x by $f(x) = e^{2x} - 2$.

(a)   Evaluate $f(\ln 3)$. [4]

....
....
....
....

(b)   Find the value of x for which $f(x) = 0$. [4]

....
....
....
....
....
....

(c) Sketch the graph of $y = e^{2x} - 2$, and clearly label all the points of intersection with the axes and asymptote. [4]

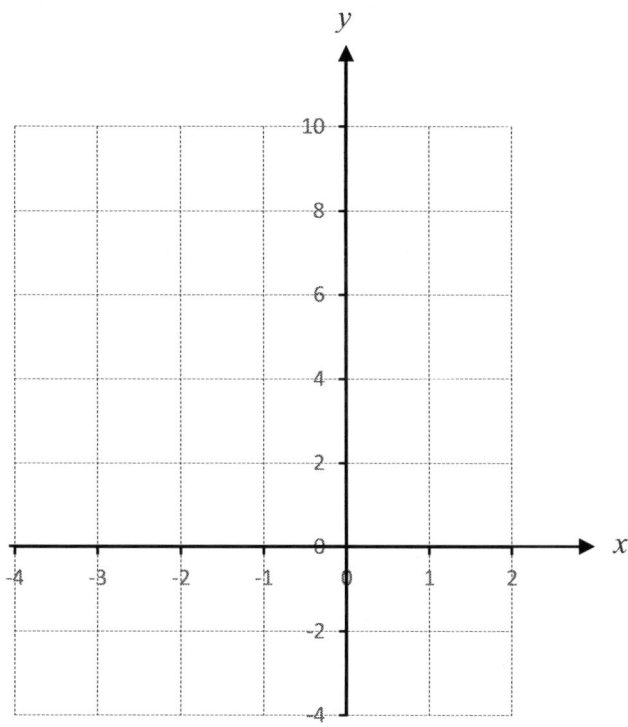

(d) Determine the inverse function $f^{-1}(x)$. [4]

10 [Maximum mark: 12]

The curve C has equation $y = 1 + x^2 - 32\sqrt{x}$, $x \geq 0$.

(a) Find the equation of the tangent to C at the point $(1, -30)$. Give your answer in the form $ax + by + c = 0$, where a, b and c are positive integers. [4]

(b) (i) Determine the coordinates of the stationary point on C. [4]

(ii) Prove that this point is a minimum turning point. [4]

Paper 2

Section A – Short questions

1   [Maximum mark: 6]

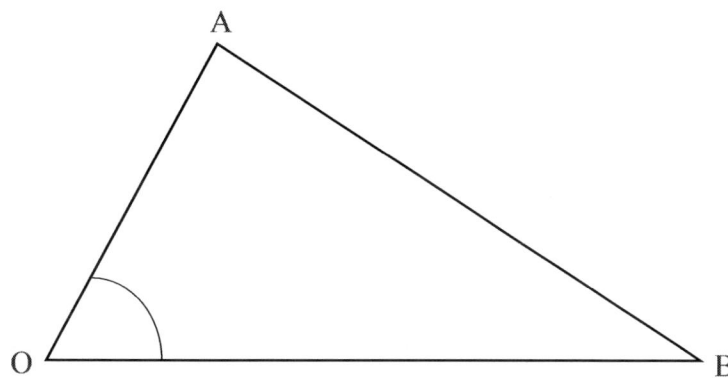

The diagram shows triangle OAB, with OA = 4 cm, OB = 6 cm and AB = $2\sqrt{7}$ cm.

(a)   Find the exact size of angle AOB.   [3]

(b)   Find the area of triangle OAB.   [3]

2   [Maximum mark: 6]

Here is a circle touching a right-angled triangle. $\hat{A} = 30°$ and the radius of the circle is r cm.

Work out the perimeter of the triangle. Give your answer in terms of r.

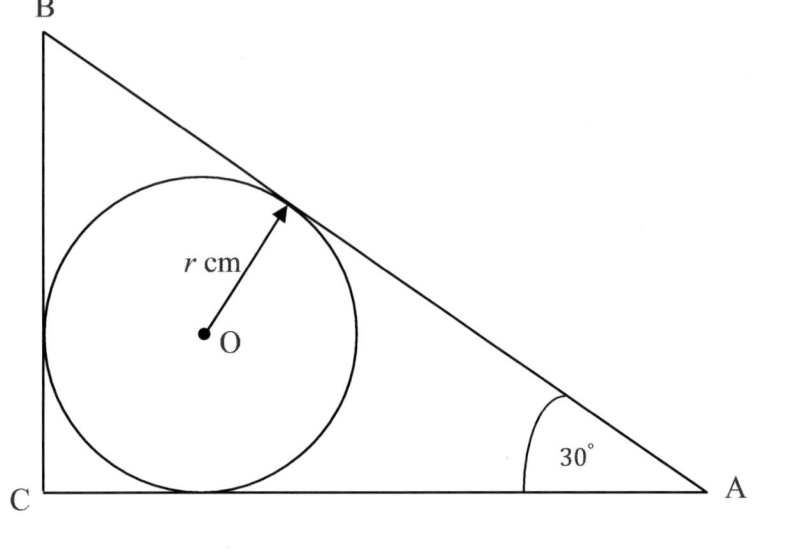

....
....
....
....
....
....
....
....

3   [Maximum mark: 5]

a, b, c and d are consecutive integers.

Prove that $ab + cd$ is always even.

....
....
....
....
....
....

4   [Maximum mark: 6]

A team of four is to be chosen from a group of five boys and four girls.

(a) Find the number of different possible teams that could be chosen. [3]

(b) Find the number of different possible teams that could be chosen, given that the team must include at least one girl and at least one boy. [3]

5   [Maximum mark: 5]

The first four terms of a geometric progression are

2   8   32   128

Work out an expression, in terms of n, for the nth term.

6   [Maximum mark: 6]

(a) Show that the equation $2\sin^2 x + \cos x = 1$ may be written in the form $2\cos^2 x - \cos x - 1 = 0$. [2]

(b) Hence, solve the equation $2\sin^2 x + \cos x = 1$, $0 \leq x \leq 2\pi$. [4]

7   [Maximum mark: 6]

Consider the following set of data: 3, 6, 1, 5, a, b, where $a > b$. The mode of this data is 5. The median of this data is 4.5.

(a) Find the value of a and the value of b. [4]

(b) Find the mean of this data. [2]

Section B – Long questions

8 [Maximum mark: 12]

(a) On the same diagram, sketch the graphs of the parabola P with equation $y = x^2$ and the line L with equation $y = 0.75x + 0.25$. [2]

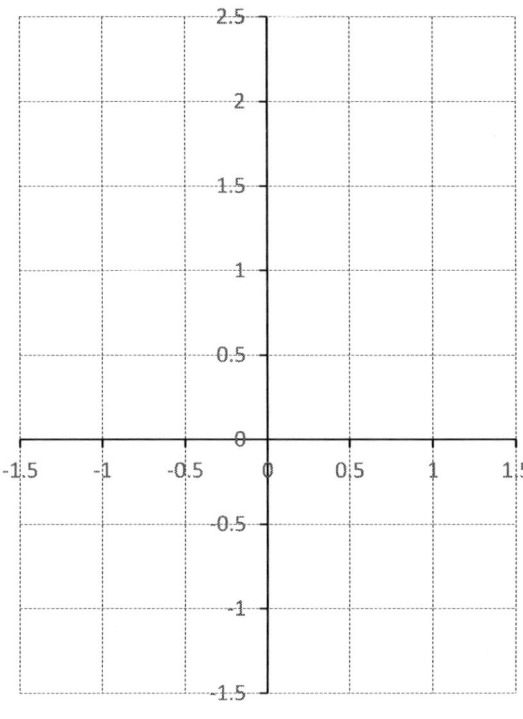

....
....
....
....

(b) P and L intersect at the points U(a, b) and V(c, d), where a < c.
Find the values of a, b, c and d. [2]

....
....
....
....

(c) Let T_1 be the tangent to P at U. Find the equation of T_1 in the form $y = mx + c$. [2]

(d) Find also the equation of T_2 the tangent to P at V. [2]

(e) Determine the coordinates of the point of intersection of T_1 and T_2. [2]

(f) Let N be the normal to P at V. Show that N is parallel to T_1. [2]

9 [Maximum mark: 18]

This question asks you to investigate the behaviour and key features of cubic polynomials of the form $4x^3 - mx^2 + k$.

A function f is defined by the formula: $f(x) = 4x^3 - 6x^2$, for $x \in \mathbb{R}$.

(a) Find the stationary points of the function $y = f(x)$ and determine their nature. [2]

(b) Find the roots of $f(x)$. [2]

(c) Sketch the graph of f. [2]

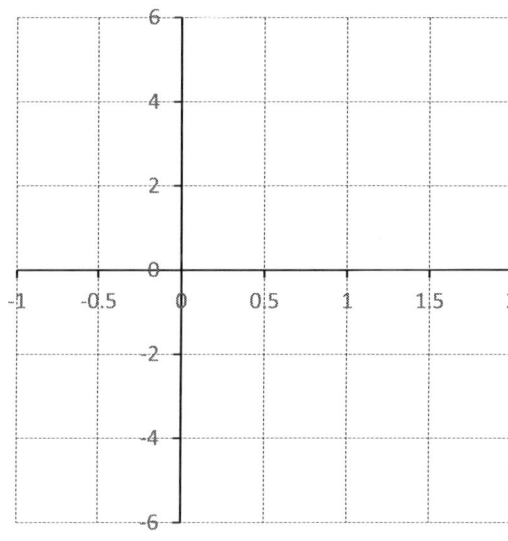

(d) A function h is defined by the formula $h(x) = 4x^3 - 6x^2 + 2$. On the same diagram as part (c) sketch $y = h(x)$ showing where it cuts the y-axis. [2]

....

....

....

....

(e) A function p is defined by the formula $p(x) = 4x^3 - 6x^2 + k$

where k is a real number.

(i) State the range of values of k, the graph of $y = p(x)$ has exactly one x-axis intercept. [2]

....

....

....

....

(ii) State the range of values of k, the graph of $y = p(x)$ has exactly two x-axis intercepts. [2]

....

....

....

....

(iii) State the range of values of k, the graph of $y = p(x)$ has exactly three x-axis intercepts. [2]

....

....

....

....

(f) A function g is defined by the formula $g(x) = 4x^3 - mx^2 + k$, where k and m are real numbers.

(i) State the value of m, the graph of $y = g(x)$ has a point of inflexion with zero gradient, and give the coordinates of the point of inflexion. [2]

(ii) State the range of values of m, the graph of $y = g(x)$ has one local maximum point and one local minimum point, and the coordinates of the local maximum and minimum. [2]

10. [Maximum mark: 10]

The velocity of a particle, v m s^{-1}, at time t seconds is given by $v = 0.3t^2 - 2.4t + 3.6$. The graph of v against t, for $0 \leq t \leq 8$, is shown below.

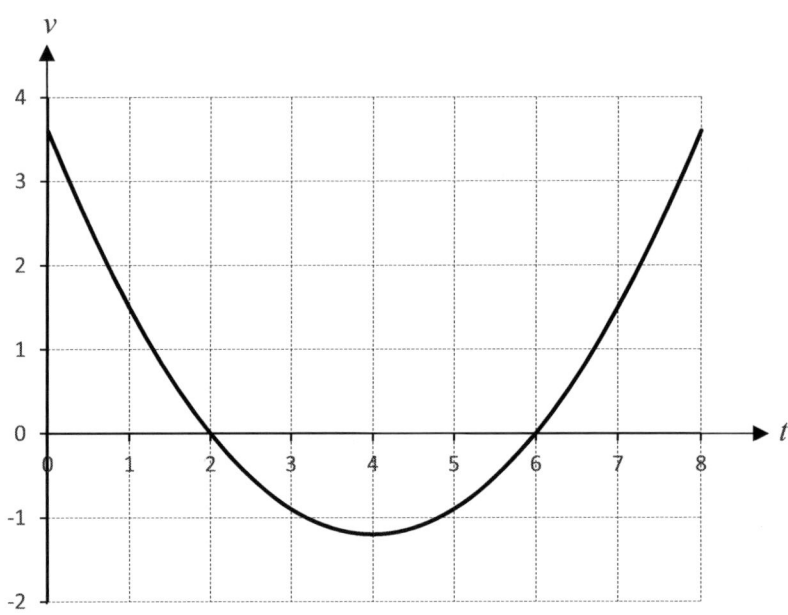

(a) Find the times when the particle stops. [2]

(b) Find the time when the particle move to the left. [2]

(c) Find the times when the particle move to the right. [2]

(d) Find the time when the acceleration is 2.4 m s^{-2}. [1]

(e) What is the displacement of the particle from the starting position when $t = 3$ seconds? [1]

....
....

(f) Find the distance travelled by the particle in the first 3 seconds. [2]

....
....
....
....
....
....
....

Paper 3

Section A – Short questions

1   [Maximum mark: 6]

PQRS is a trapezium, as shown in the diagram. $\widehat{SPQ} = 60°$. RQ is perpendicular to SR and PQ.

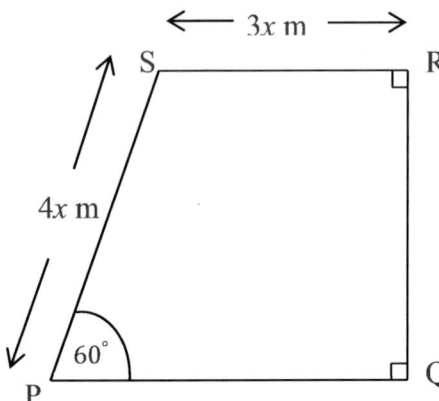

Diagram **NOT** accurately drawn

Work out the area of the trapezium, in terms of x.

2   [Maximum mark: 6]

The shape consists of two overlapping circles below. C_1 and C_2 are centres of the circles.

Find the perimeter of this shape.

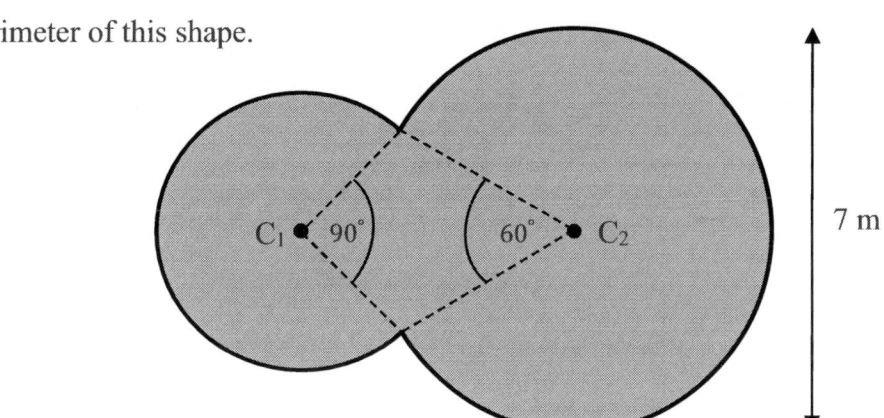

Give your answer in terms of π.

....
....
....
....
....

3   [Maximum mark: 6]

(a) Show that $\log_4(\cos 2x + 2) = \log_2 \sqrt{\cos 2x + 2}$.   [3]

....
....
....
....

(b) Hence or otherwise solve $\log_2(2\cos x) = \log_4(\cos 2x + 2)$ for $0 < x < \pi$.   [3]

....
....
....
....
....

4 [Maximum mark: 6]

Two unbiased tetrahedral (four-sided) dice with faces labelled 1, 2, 3, 4 are thrown and the scores recorded. Let the random variables T be the minimum of these two scores. The probability distribution of T is given in the following table.

t	1	2	3	4
$P(T=t)$	$\dfrac{7}{16}$	a	b	$\dfrac{1}{16}$

(a) Find the value of a and the value of b. [4]

(b) Find the expected value of T. [2]

5   [Maximum mark: 6]

A given polynomial function is defined as $f(x) = a_0 + a_1 x + a_2 x^2 + \cdots + a_n x^n$.

The roots of the polynomial equation $f(x) = 0$ are consecutive terms of a geometric sequence with a common ratio of 0.5 and first term 2.

Given that $a_{n-1} = -15$ and $a_n = 4$ find

(a) the degree of the polynomial; [3]

(b) the value of a_0. [3]

6   [Maximum mark: 4]

(a) Find $\int \cos^2(x)\, dx$. [2]

(b) Hence, evaluate $\int_0^{\frac{\pi}{4}} \cos^2(x)\, dx$. [2]

7	[Maximum mark: 6]

A set of 10 student group has a mean mass of 70 kg. A new student called Steve joins this group. The new mean mass of the 11 students is now 72 kg.

(a)	Find Steve's mass. [3]

(b)	The new lower quartile and upper quartile for the masses of the 11 students are 66 kg and 76 kg respectively. Determine whether Steve's mass is an outlier, and justify your answer. [3]

Section B – Long questions

8	[Maximum mark: 12]

(a)	On a single diagram, sketch the curve $y = 8x - x^2$ and the line $y = ax$, where $0 < a < 8$. [4]

(b) (i) Show that the area of the finite region enclosed between the curve and the line is $\dfrac{(8-a)^3}{6}$. [4]

(ii) Given that this area is exactly one-eighth the area enclosed between the curve and the x-axis, determine the exact value of a. [4]

9. [Maximum mark: 15]

The heights in metres of a random sample of 80 cows in a field were measured and the following cumulative frequency graph obtained.

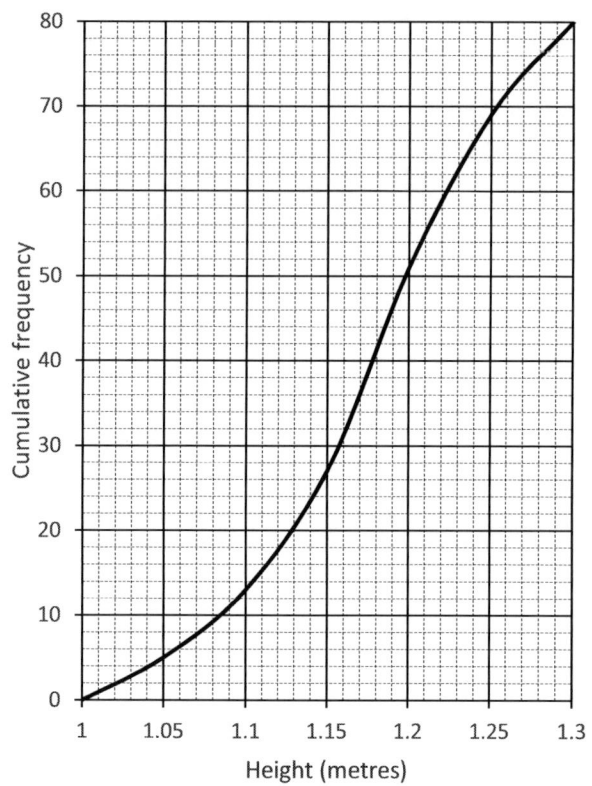

(a) Estimate the median of these data. [2]

....
....

(b) Estimate the interquartile range for these data. [3]

....
....
....
....

(c) Draw a box-and-whisker diagram to summarize information of these data. [3]

(d) Draw a frequency table for the heights of the cows, using a class width of 0.05 metres. [3]

(e) A cow is selected at random.
 (i) Find the probability that its height is less than or equal to 1.15 metres. [2]

 ....
 ....
 ....
 ....

 (ii) Given that its height is less than or equal to 1.15 metres, find the probability that its height is less than or equal to 1.12 metres. [2]

 ....
 ....
 ....
 ....
 ....
 ....
 ....
 ....

10   [Maximum mark: 13]

Let $f(x) = x^3 - 6x^2 + 9x + 4$

(a) Find $f'(x)$. [2]

(b) Sketch the graph of $y = f'(x)$, indicating clearly the coordinates of minimum point, the x-axis intercepts, and the y-axis intercept. [3]

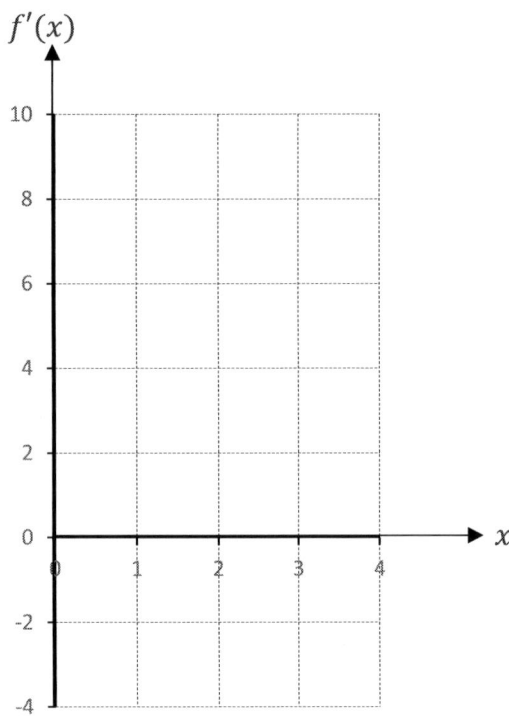

(c) Find all values of x for which $f(x)$ is increasing. [2]

(d) Find $f''(x)$. [2]

....

....

(e) Hence find and classify the stationary points on the graph of $y = f(x)$. [2]

....

....

....

....

(f) The equation $f(x) = k$ has three solutions. Find the possible values of k. [2]

....

....

....

....

Paper 4

Section A – Short questions

1   [Maximum mark: 6]

A tunnel entrance has centre C and a circular arc of diameter 20 metres. The height of the tunnel entrance is 16 metres.

Work out the width of road surface (*w*) of the tunnel.

2 [Maximum mark: 6]

Here are a sphere and a cone. The base of the cone and the sphere have the same radius r cm. l, the slant height, is $\sqrt{17}r$ cm.

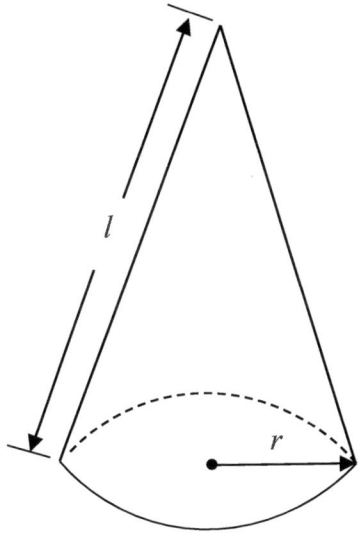
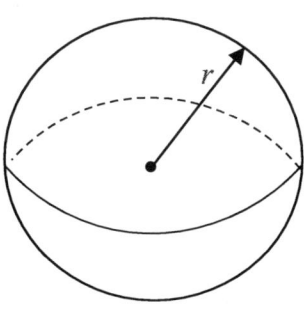

Prove that the sphere and the cone have the same volume.

3 [Maximum mark: 5]

Solve $|2x + 1| = x^2 - 2$, where $x \in \mathbb{R}$.

4 [Maximum mark: 6]

A bag contains three counters numbered 1, 2 and 3 respectively. John selects one of these counters at random and he notes the number on the selected counter. He then tosses that number of fair coins.

(a) Calculate the probability that no head is obtained. [3]

(b) Given that no head is obtained, find the probability that he tossed two coins. [3]

5   [Maximum mark: 5]

In the expansion of $(x+1)(x+p)^6$, where $p \in \mathbb{R}$, the coefficient of the term in x^5 is 21.

Find the possible values of p.

6   [Maximum mark: 6]

Given that $\int_{-3}^{3} f(x)dx = 12$ and $\int_{0}^{3} f(x)dx = 15$, find

(a) $\int_{-3}^{0} (f(x)+3)dx$ [3]

(b) $\int_{-3}^{0} f(x+3)dx$ [3]

7   [Maximum mark: 6]

A cylinder of radius r is inscribed in a sphere with centre O and radius R as shown in the following diagram. The height of the cylinder is h, X denotes the centre of its base and B a point where the cylinder touches the sphere.

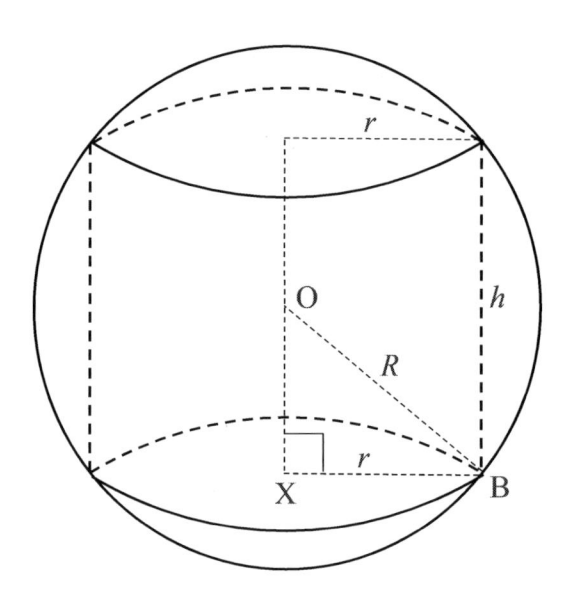

(a) Show that the volume of the cylinder may be expressed by $V = \dfrac{\pi}{4}(4R^2h - h^3)$. [3]

(b) Given that there is one inscribed cylinder having a maximum volume, show that the volume of this cylinder is $\dfrac{4\sqrt{3}\pi R^3}{9}$. [3]

Section B – Long questions

8   [Maximum mark: 8]

(a)   Sketch the graph of $f(x) = \dfrac{x+3}{2x+1}$, stating equations of any asymptotes and the coordinates of any points of intersection with the axes.   [4]

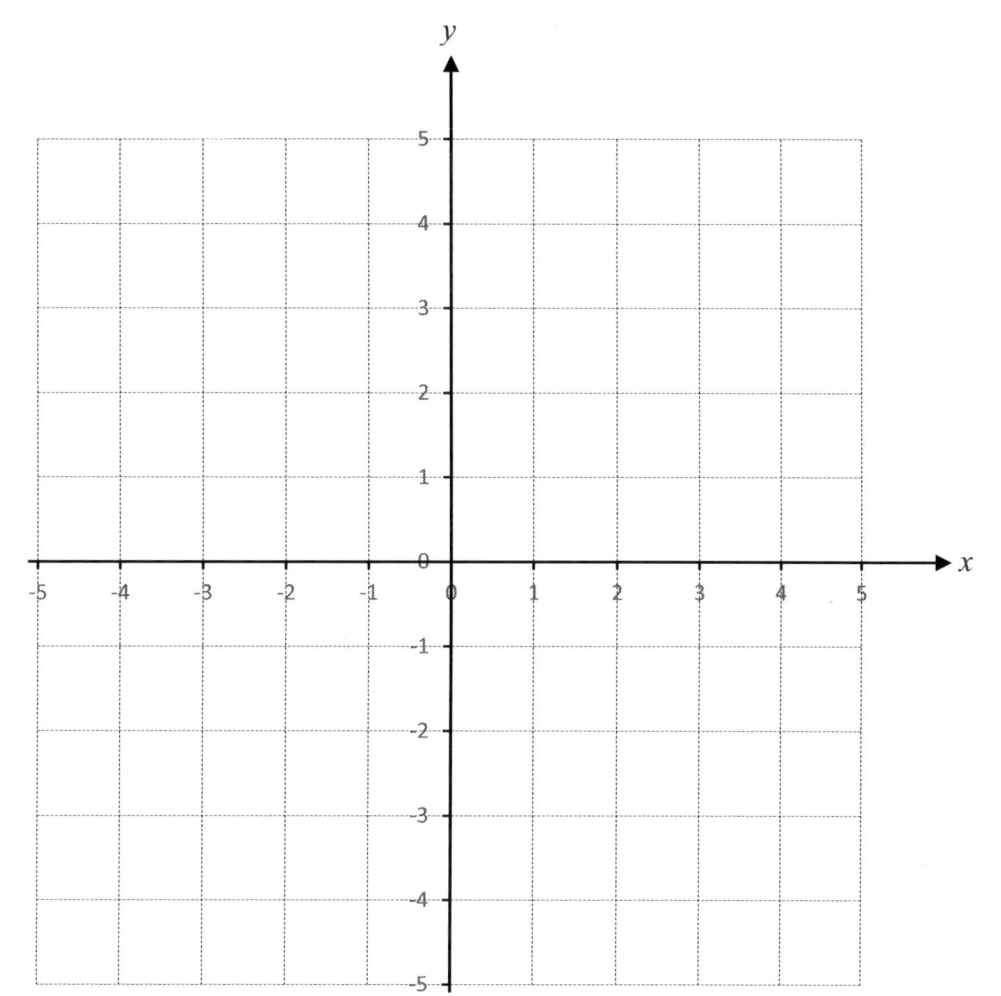

(b) Consider the function $g: x \to \sqrt{\dfrac{x+3}{2x+1}}$

Write down

(i) the largest possible domain of g; [2]

(ii) the corresponding range of g. [2]

10 [Maximum mark: 17]

Given that $f(x) = 3xe^{-x}$ for $-3 \leq x \leq 3$

(a) Show that $f(x)$ has one turning point and one point of inflection. [4]

(b) Identify the nature of the turning point and state its coordinates. [2]

(c) Find the coordinates of the point of inflection and hence sketch the graph of $f(x)$. [4]

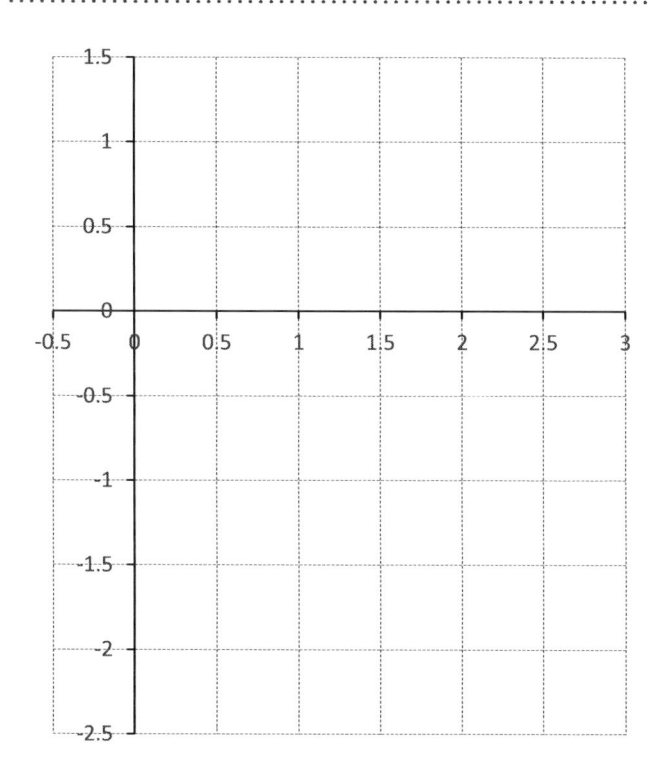

(d) Find the equation of the tangent to the curve at the point of inflection. [2]

....

....

....

....

....

....

(e) Determine the coordinates of the tangent where this tangent meets the x-axis. [2]

....

....

....

(f) Calculate the area bounded by this tangent and the x- and y-axes. [3]

....

....

....

....

Paper 1 solutions

Section A – Short questions

1 [Maximum mark: 5]

Here is a triangle. $\sin x = \dfrac{3\sqrt{3}}{8}$

Diagram **NOT** accurately drawn

Work out the value of y.

$\dfrac{BC}{\sin \hat{A}} = \dfrac{AB}{\sin \hat{C}} \Rightarrow \dfrac{y}{\sin x} = \dfrac{20}{\sin 60°} \Rightarrow y = \dfrac{20 \times \dfrac{3\sqrt{3}}{8}}{\dfrac{\sqrt{3}}{2}} = 15$

2 [Maximum mark: 5]

ABC is an equilateral triangle. A, B and C are on the circumference of a circle. The length of a side of the equilateral triangle is x cm.

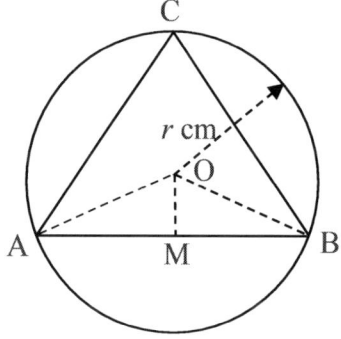

Work out the value of the radius of the circle.

Give your answer in terms of x.

$r = OB = \dfrac{AB}{2} \div \cos \widehat{MBO} = \dfrac{x}{2} \div \cos 30° = \dfrac{x}{2} \div \dfrac{\sqrt{3}}{2} = \dfrac{\sqrt{3}x}{3}$

3 [Maximum mark: 5]

Consider two consecutive integers, n and $n+1$.

Prove that the sum of the squares of any two consecutive integers is odd.

$n^2 + (n+1)^2 = n^2 + n^2 + 2n + 1 = 2(n^2 + n) + 1$

$2(n^2 + n) + 1$ is old, therefore the sum of the squares of any two consecutive integers is odd.

4	[Maximum mark: 6]

The events A and B are such that $P(A) = 0.3$, $P(B) = 0.5$ and $P(A \cap B) = 0.2$. Find the following probabilities:

(a)	$P(A \cup B)$;	[3]

$P(A \cup B) = P(A) + P(B) - P(A \cap B) = 0.3 + 0.5 - 0.2 = 0.6$

(b)	$P(A|B)$.	[3]

$P(A|B) = \dfrac{P(A \cap B)}{P(B)} = \dfrac{0.2}{0.5} = 0.4$

5	[Maximum mark: 6]

Let a_n denote the nth term of an arithmetic sequence, and S_n the sum of its first n terms.

(a)	Given that $a_3 = 19$ and $S_{25} = 100$, work out the first term and the common difference.	[3]

$19 = a_1 + 2d$ 	(1)

$100 = 25 \times \dfrac{2a_1 + 24d}{2} \Rightarrow 4 = a_1 + 12d$ 	(2)

Eqs. (1) – (2) $\Rightarrow 15 = -10d \Rightarrow$

$d = -\dfrac{3}{2}$

From Eq. (1),

$a_1 = 19 - 2d = 19 - 2 \times \left(-\dfrac{3}{2}\right) = 22$

(b)	Find the least number of terms required for which $S_n < 0$.	[3]

$S_n = \dfrac{n\left(2 \times 22 + (n-1) \times \left(-\dfrac{3}{2}\right)\right)}{2} < 0$

Since $n > 0$, we have that

$2 \times 22 + (n-1) \times \left(-\dfrac{3}{2}\right) < 0 \Rightarrow 88 - 3n + 3 < 0 \Rightarrow n > \dfrac{91}{3}$

Therefore the least number of terms required for which $S_n < 0$, is 31.

6   [Maximum mark: 6]

The function f and g are defined such that $f(x) = \dfrac{(x+3)^2}{4}$ and $g(x) = 8x - 2$.

(a)   Show that $(g \circ f)(x) = 2(x+2)(x+4)$.   [3]

$$(g \circ f)(x) = g\left(\dfrac{(x+3)^2}{4}\right) = 8 \times \dfrac{(x+3)^2}{4} - 2 = 2(x+3)^2 - 2$$

$$= 2(x+3-1)(x+3+1) = 2(x+2)(x+4)$$

Therefore $(g \circ f)(x) = 2(x+2)(x+4)$

(b)   Given that $(g \circ f)^{-1}(a) = 3$, find the value of a.   [3]

$(g \circ f)^{-1}(a) = 3 \Rightarrow a = 2(3+2)(3+4) = 70$

Therefore $a = 70$

7   [Maximum mark: 5]

A curve has equation $y = x^2 + 4x + 4$.

The tangent to the curve at point P on the curve is perpendicular to the line $y = -\dfrac{1}{2}x + 5$.

Work out the coordinates of P.

The coordinates of P are $(a, a^2 + 4a + 4)$.

$\dfrac{dy}{dx} = 2x + 4 = 2a + 4$

The tangent to the curve at point P on the curve is perpendicular to the line $y = -\dfrac{1}{2}x + 5$

$\therefore 2a + 4 = 2 \Rightarrow a = -1$, $a^2 + 4a + 4 = (-1)^2 + 4 \times (-1) + 4 = 1$

The coordinates of P are (-1, 1).

Section B – Long questions

8   [Maximum mark: 14]

The sketch shows the curve of $y = f(x)$. The curve passes through the origin O and has a local maximum at $A(1, \frac{2}{3})$ and a local minimum at B(3, 0).

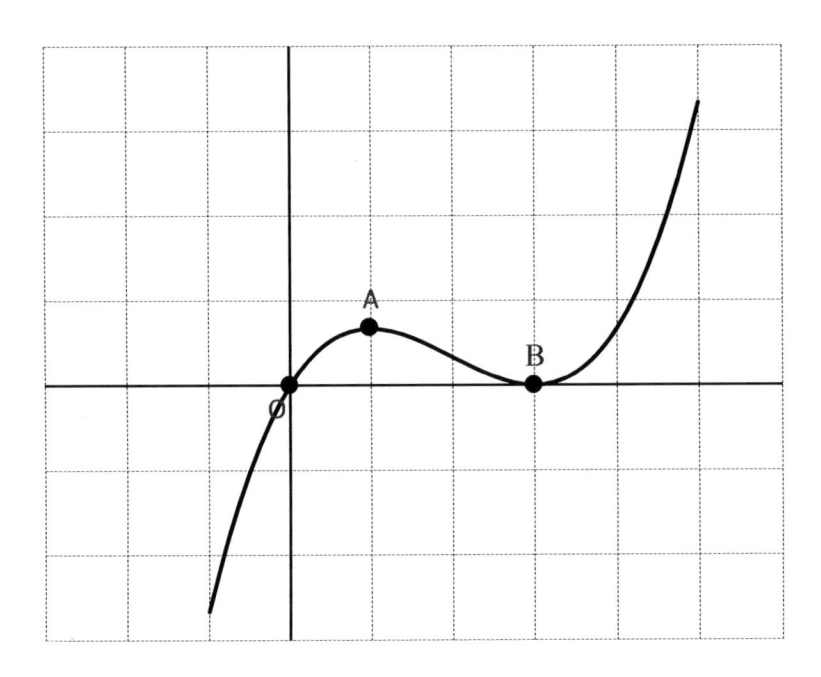

On separate diagrams, sketch the following curves, indicating clearly the coordinates of the images of the points O, A and B.

(a) $y = f(x + 1)$;   [3]

Horizontal translation, 1 unit in the negative x-direction.

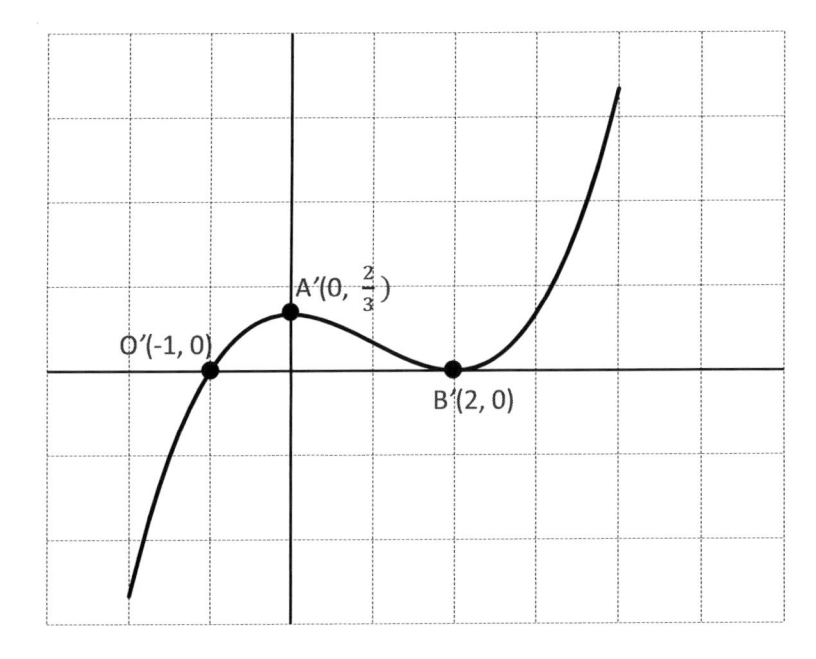

46

(b) $y = 2f(x)$; [3]

Stretch in y-direction

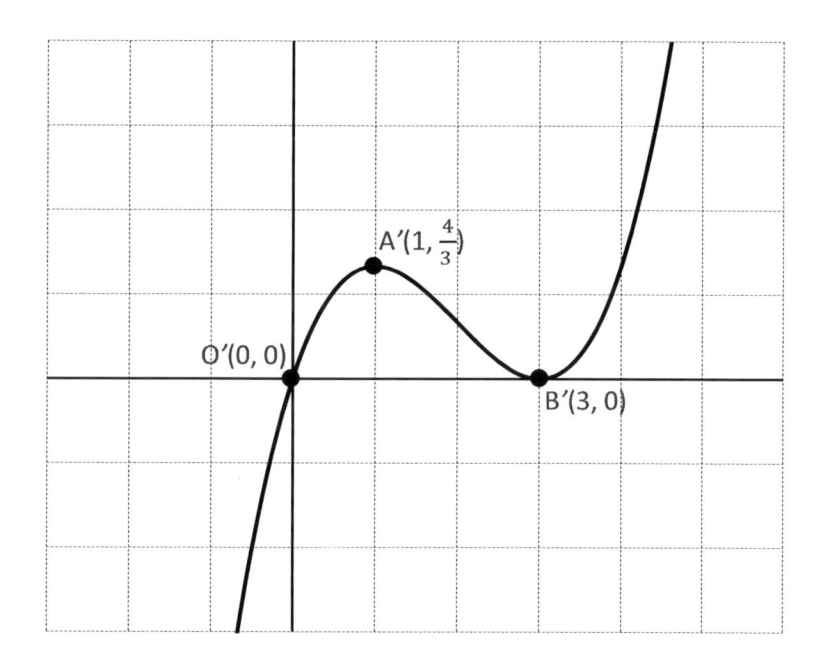

A'$(1, \frac{4}{3})$

O'$(0, 0)$

B'$(3, 0)$

(c) $y = f(2x)$; [3]

Horizontal stretch with scale factor 0.5.

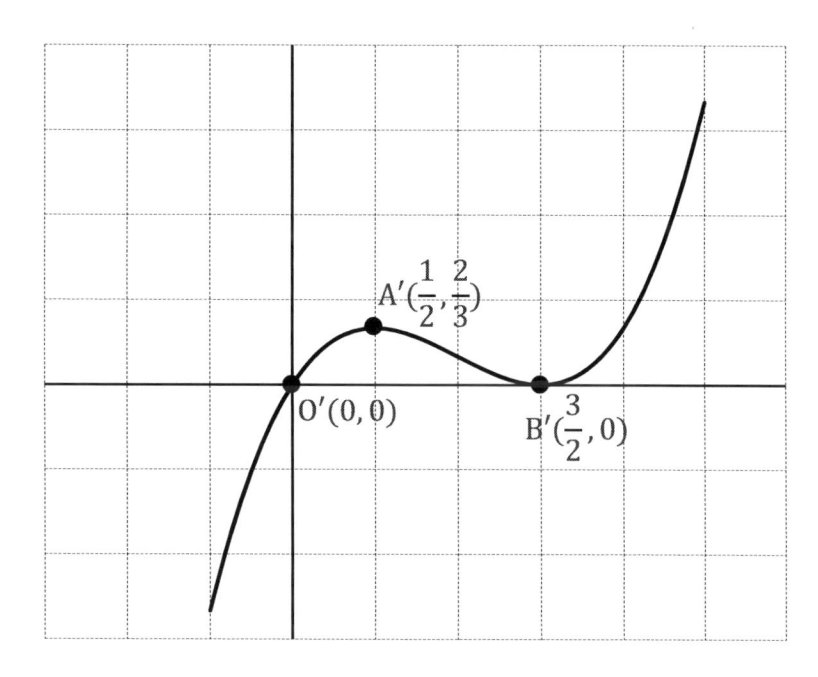

A'$(\frac{1}{2}, \frac{2}{3})$

O'$(0, 0)$

B'$(\frac{3}{2}, 0)$

(d) $y = f(2-x)$. [5]

Reflection in a vertical line, $x = 1$

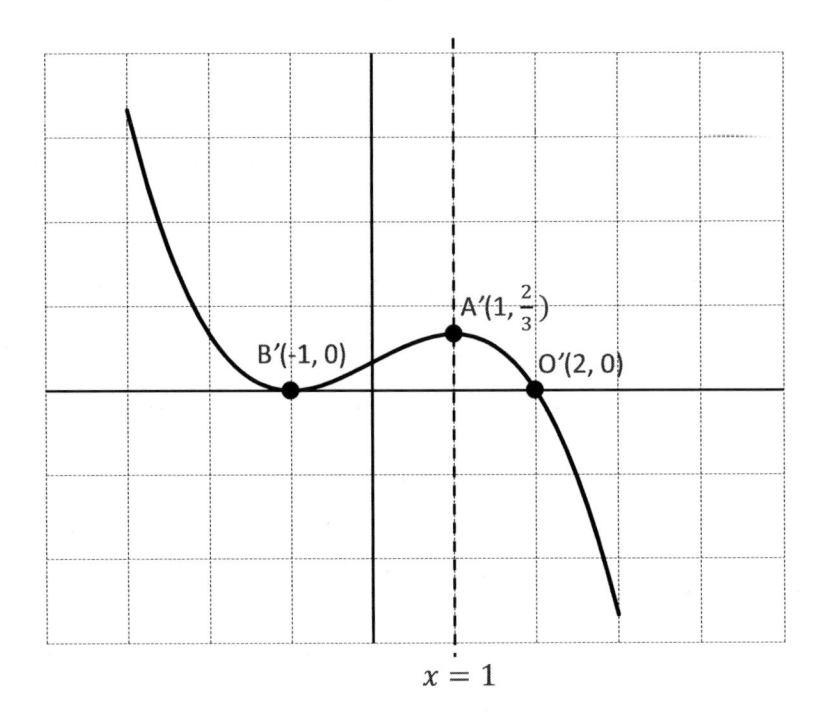

[Graph showing curve with points B'(-1, 0), A'(1, 2/3), O'(2, 0), and dashed line x = 1]

9   [Maximum mark: 16]

The function f is defined for all x by $f(x) = e^{2x} - 2$

(a) Evaluate $f(\ln 3)$. [4]

$f(\ln 3) = e^{2\ln 3} - 2 = e^{\ln 9} - 2 = 9 - 2 = 7$

(b) Find the value of x for which $f(x) = 0$. [4]

$e^{2x} - 2 = 0 \Rightarrow e^{2x} = 2 \Rightarrow 2x = \ln 2 \Rightarrow x = \dfrac{\ln 2}{2}$

(c) Sketch the graph of $y = e^{2x} - 2$, and clearly label all the points of intersection with the axes and asymptote. [4]

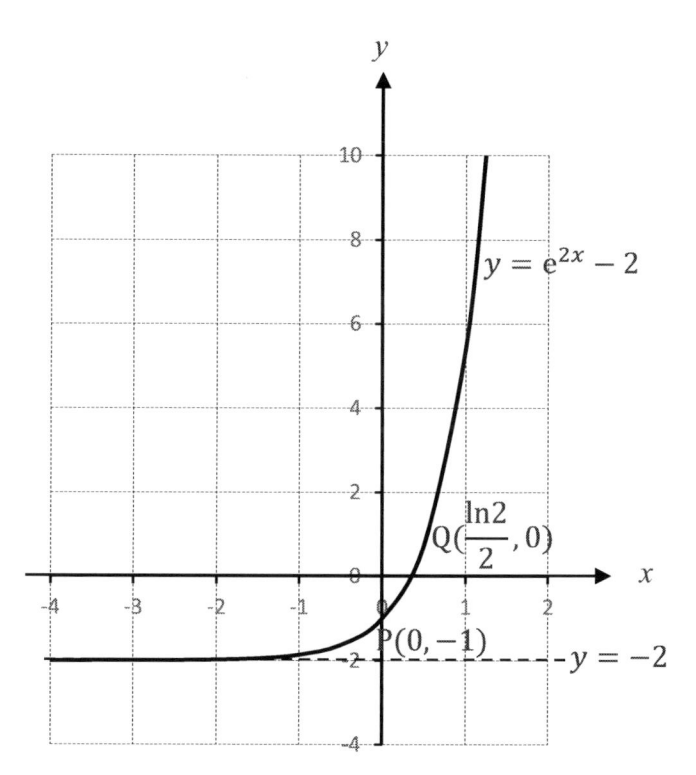

The horizontal asymptote is $y = -2$

The curve intersects the x-axis at $Q\left(\frac{\ln 2}{2}, 0\right)$, and the y-axis at $P(0, -1)$.

(d) Determine the inverse function $f^{-1}(x)$. [4]

$x = e^{2y} - 2 \Rightarrow x + 2 = e^{2y} \Rightarrow \ln(x + 2) = 2y \Rightarrow y = \dfrac{\ln(x + 2)}{2}$ for the domain $x > -2$

10 [Maximum mark: 12]

The curve C has equation $y = 1 + x^2 - 32\sqrt{x}$, $x \geq 0$.

(a) Find the equation of the tangent to C at the point $(1, -30)$. Give your answer in the form $ax + by + c = 0$, where a, b and c are positive integers. [4]

$\dfrac{dy}{dx} = 2x - \dfrac{16}{\sqrt{x}} = 2 \times 1 - \dfrac{16}{\sqrt{1}} = -14$, when $x = 1$

The equation of the tangent to the curve at the point (1, -30) can be obtained as follows:

$y + 30 = -14(x - 1) \Rightarrow 14x + y + 16 = 0$

(b) (i) Determine the coordinates of the stationary point on C. [4]

$$\frac{dy}{dx} = 2x - \frac{16}{\sqrt{x}} = 0 \Rightarrow x^{\frac{3}{2}} = 8 \Rightarrow x = 4$$

$$y = 1 + 4^2 - 32\sqrt{4} = -47$$

The coordinates of the stationary point on the curve are (4, -47).

(ii) Prove that this point is a minimum turning point. [4]

$$\frac{d^2y}{dx^2} = 2 + 8x^{-\frac{3}{2}} = 2 + 8 \times 4^{-\frac{3}{2}} = 3 > 0, \text{ when } x = 4$$

Therefore the stationary point on the curve is a minimum turning point.

Paper 2 solutions

Section A – Short questions

1 [Maximum mark: 6]

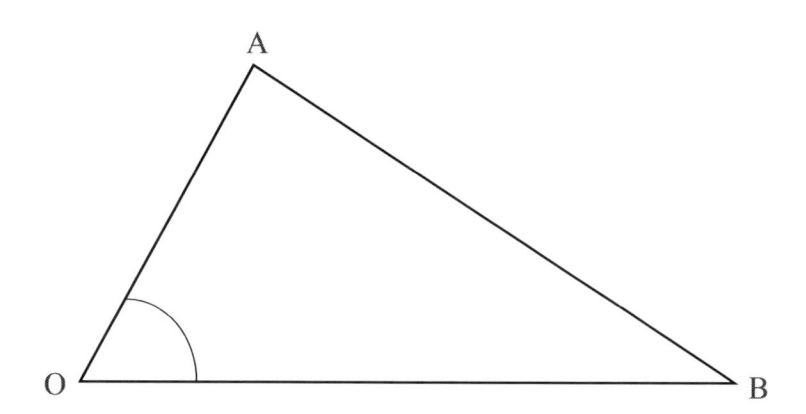

The diagram shows triangle OAB, with OA = 4 cm, OB = 6 cm and AB = $2\sqrt{7}$ cm.

(a) Find the exact size of angle AOB. [3]

$AB^2 = OA^2 + OB^2 - 2 \times OA \times OB \times \cos\theta$

$$\Rightarrow \cos\theta = \frac{OA^2 + OB^2 - AB^2}{2 \times OA \times OB} = \frac{16 + 36 - 28}{2 \times 4 \times 6} = \frac{1}{2}$$

Angle AOB is $\frac{\pi}{3}$ or $60°$

(b) Find the area of triangle OAB. [3]

The area of triangle OAB is

$$\frac{OA \times OB \times \sin\theta}{2} = \frac{4 \times 6 \times \frac{\sqrt{3}}{2}}{2} = 6\sqrt{3} \text{ cm}^2$$

2   [Maximum mark: 6]

Here is a circle touching a right-angled triangle. $\hat{A} = 30°$ and the radius of the circle is r cm.

Work out the perimeter of the triangle. Give your answer in terms of r.

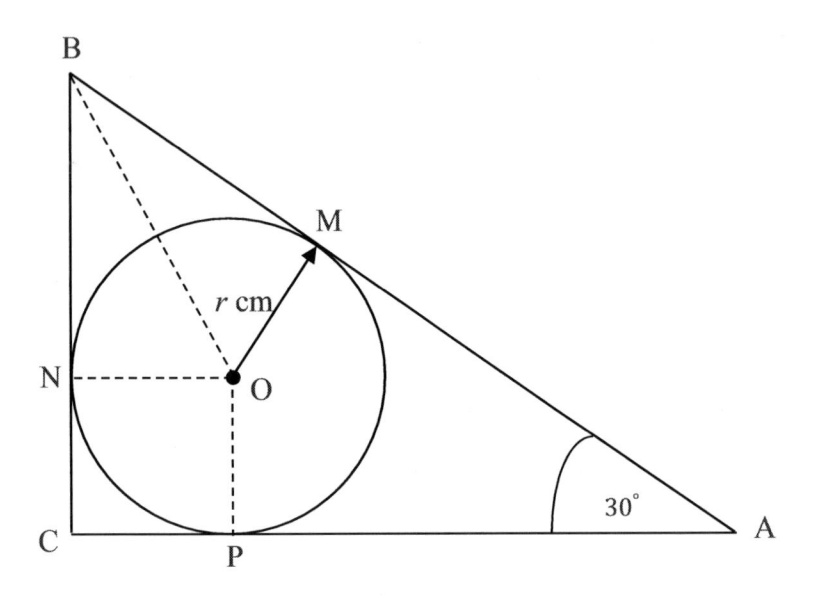

$\hat{A} = 30° \Rightarrow \hat{B} = 90° - 30° = 60°, \widehat{OBM} = 30°$

$BN = BM = \dfrac{OM}{\tan \widehat{OBM}} = \dfrac{r}{\tan 30°} = \sqrt{3}r$

$BC = BN + NC = \sqrt{3}r + r, AB = \dfrac{BC}{\sin 30°} = 2BC = 2\sqrt{3}r + 2r$

$AC = AB \cos 30° = (2\sqrt{3}r + 2r) \times \dfrac{\sqrt{3}}{2} = 3r + \sqrt{3}r$

The perimeter of the triangle is calculated as follows:

$AC + AB + BC = (3r + \sqrt{3}r) + (2\sqrt{3}r + 2r) + (\sqrt{3}r + r) = (6r + 4\sqrt{3}r)$ cm

3   [Maximum mark: 5]

a, b, c and d are consecutive integers.

Prove that $ab + cd$ is always even.

$b = a + 1, c = a + 2, d = a + 3$

$ab + cd = a(a+1) + (a+2)(a+3) = a^2 + a + a^2 + 5a + 6 = 2(a^2 + 3a + 3)$

$2(a^2 + 3a + 3)$ is always even when a is an integer, therefore $ab + cd$ is always even.

4   [Maximum mark: 6]

A team of four is to be chosen from a group of five boys and four girls.

(a)   Find the number of different possible teams that could be chosen.   [3]

$$^9C_4 = \frac{9!}{4!\,5!} = 126$$

(b)   Find the number of different possible teams that could be chosen, given that the team must include at least one girl and at least one boy.   [3]

The number of different possible teams that could be chosen, given that the team includes 4 boys, is:

$$^5C_4 = \frac{5!}{4!\,1!} = 5$$

The number of different possible teams that could be chosen, given that the team includes 4 girls, is:

$$^4C_4 = \frac{4!}{4!\,0!} = 1$$

The number of different possible teams that could be chosen, given that the team must include at least one girl and at least one boy, is:

$$^9C_4 - {^5C_4} - {^4C_4} = 126 - 5 - 1 = 120$$

Another method: 3 boys 1 girl, 2 boys 2 girls, and 1 boy 3 girls are chosen, the number of different possible teams can be calculated as follows.

$$^5C_3\,{^4C_1} + {^5C_2}\,{^4C_2} + {^5C_1}\,{^4C_3} = 120$$

5   [Maximum mark: 5]

The first four terms of a geometric progression are

2   8   32   128

Work out an expression, in terms of n, for the nth term.

$$a_2 = a_1 r,\ r = \frac{a_2}{a_1} = \frac{8}{2} = 4,\ a_n = a_1 r^{n-1},\ a_n = 2 \times 4^{n-1}$$

6 [Maximum mark: 6]

(a) Show that the equation $2\sin^2 x + \cos x = 1$ may be written in the form
$2\cos^2 x - \cos x - 1 = 0$. [2]

$2\sin^2 x + \cos x = 1 \Rightarrow 2(1 - \cos^2 x) + \cos x = 1 \Rightarrow 2\cos^2 x - \cos x - 1 = 0$

(b) Hence, solve the equation $2\sin^2 x + \cos x = 1$, $0 \leq x \leq 2\pi$. [4]

$2\sin^2 x + \cos x = 1 \Rightarrow 2\cos^2 x - \cos x - 1 = 0 \Rightarrow (2\cos x + 1)(\cos x - 1) = 0$

$2\cos x + 1 = 0 \Rightarrow x = \dfrac{2\pi}{3}, \dfrac{4\pi}{3}$

$\cos x - 1 = 0 \Rightarrow x = 0, 2\pi$

So $x = 0, \dfrac{2\pi}{3}, \dfrac{4\pi}{3}, 2\pi$

7 [Maximum mark: 6]

Consider the following set of data: 3, 6, 1, 5, a, b, where $a > b$. The mode of this data is 5. The median of this data is 4.5.

(a) Find the value of a and the value of b. [4]

As the mode is 5, there must be at least another 5. So we have 1, 3, 5, 5, 6 with another number to be placed in order. The median will be the average of the 3rd and 4th places of data. Since the median of this data is 4.5, the missing number of data must be a 4. Thus $a = 5, b = 4$.

(b) Find the mean of this data. [2]

$\bar{x} = \dfrac{1 + 3 + 4 + 5 + 5 + 6}{6} = 4$

Section B – Long questions

8   [Maximum mark: 12]

(a)   On the same diagram, sketch the graphs of the parabola P with equation $y = x^2$ and the line L with equation $y = 0.75x + 0.25$.   [2]

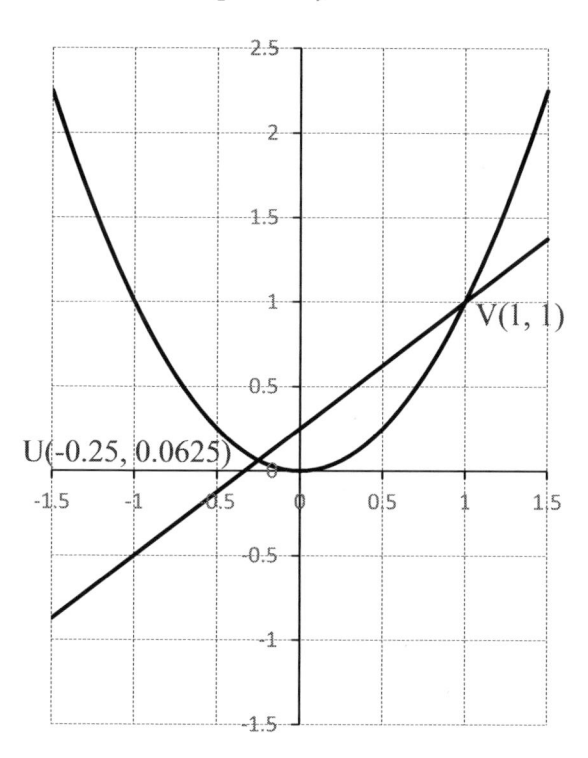

(b)   P and L intersect at the points U(a, b) and V(c, d), where $a < c$.

Find the values of a, b, c and d.   [2]

$a = -0.25, b = 0.0625, c = 1, d = 1$

(c)   Let T_1 be the tangent to P at U. Find the equation of T_1 in the form $y = mx + c$.   [2]

$\frac{dy}{dx} = 2x$

$m = 2x = 2 \times (-0.25) = -0.5$

U(-0.25, 0.0625) on line T_1

$y = mx + c \Rightarrow 0.0625 = -0.5 \times (-0.25) + c \Rightarrow c = -0.0625$

The equation of T_1 is $y = -0.5x - 0.0625$

(d) Find also the equation of T_2 the tangent to P at V. [2]

$k = 2x = 2$

V(1, 1) on line T_2

$y = kx + b \Rightarrow 1 = 2 \times (1) + b \Rightarrow b = -1$

The equation of T_2 the tangent to P at V is: $y = 2x - 1$

(e) Determine the coordinates of the point of intersection of T_1 and T_2. [2]

$y = -0.5x - 0.0625$ (1) $y = 2x - 1$ (2)

Eqs (2) – (1)

$2.5x - 1 + 0.0625 = 0 \Rightarrow x = 0.375$

$y = 2x - 1 = 2 \times 0.375 - 1 = -0.25$

The coordinates of the point of intersection of T_1 and T_2 are (0.375, -0.25)

(f) Let N be the normal to P at V. Show that N is parallel to T_1. [2]

The equation of T_2 the tangent to P at V is: $y = 2x - 1$, the gradient of N is $-\dfrac{1}{2}$.

Which is equal to the gradient of T_1. Therefore N is parallel to T_1.

9   [Maximum mark: 18]

This question asks you to investigate the behaviour and key features of cubic polynomials of the form $4x^3 - mx^2 + k$.

A function f is defined by the formula: $f(x) = 4x^3 - 6x^2$, for $x \in \mathbb{R}$.

(a) Find the stationary points of the function $y = f(x)$ and determine their nature. [2]

$f'(x) = 12x^2 - 12x = 0 \Rightarrow x(x - 1) = 0 \Rightarrow x = 0, x = 1$

$f(0) = 4 \times 0^3 - 6 \times 0^2 = 0, f(1) = 4 \times 1^3 - 6 \times 1^2 = -2$

$f''(x) = 24x - 12$

$f''(0) = 0 - 12 = -12 < 0$

$f''(1) = 24 \times 1 - 12 = 12 > 0$

(0, 0) is the maximum point and (1, -2) is the minimum point.

(b) Find the roots of $f(x)$. [2]

$4x^3 - 6x^2 = 0 \Rightarrow 2x^2(2x - 3) = 0 \Rightarrow x = 0, \dfrac{3}{2}$

(c)   Sketch the graph of f. [2]

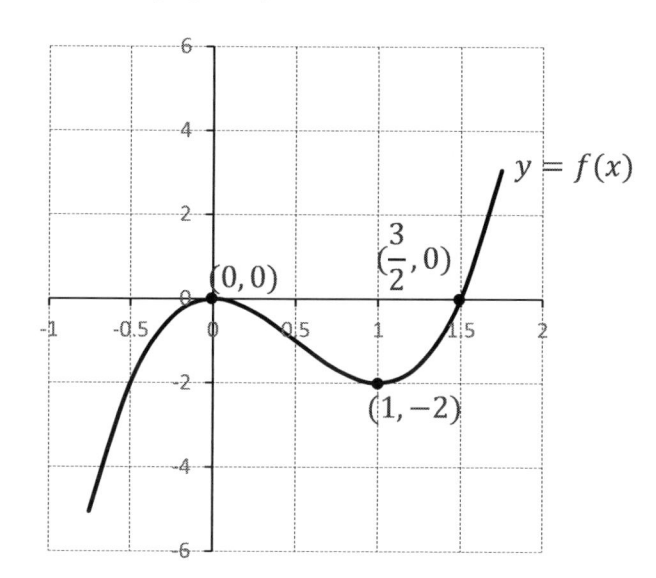

(d)   A function h is defined by the formula $h(x) = 4x^3 - 6x^2 + 2$. On the same diagram as part (c) sketch $y = h(x)$ showing where it cuts the y-axis. [2]

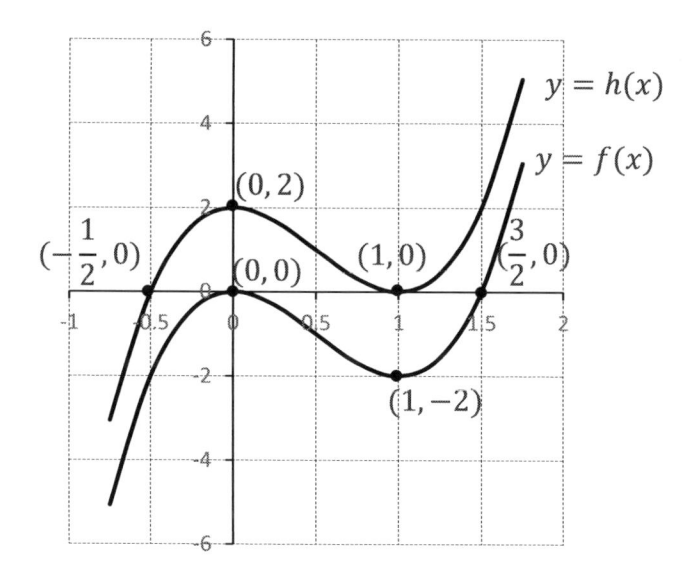

(e)   A function p is defined by the formula $p(x) = 4x^3 - 6x^2 + k$ where k is a real number.

  (i)   State the range of values of k, the graph of $y = p(x)$ has exactly one x-axis intercept. [2]

From the diagrams of $y = f(x)$ and $y = h(x)$, the graph of $y = p(x)$ has exactly one x-axis intercept, for $k < 0$ and $k > 2$.

(ii) State the range of values of k, the graph of $y = p(x)$ has exactly two x-axis intercepts. [2]

From the diagrams of $y = f(x)$ and $y = h(x)$, the graph of $y = p(x)$ has exactly two x-axis intercepts, for $k = 0$ and $k = 2$.

(iii) State the range of values of k, the graph of $y = p(x)$ has exactly three x-axis intercepts. [2]

From the diagrams of $y = f(x)$ and $y = h(x)$, the graph of $y = p(x)$ has exactly three x-axis intercepts for $0 < k < 2$.

(f) A function g is defined by the formula $g(x) = 4x^3 - mx^2 + k$, where k and m are real numbers.

(i) State the value of m, the graph of $y = g(x)$ has a point of inflexion with zero gradient, and give the coordinates of the point of inflexion. [2]

$g'(x) = 12x^2 - 2mx = 2x(6x - m)$

If $m = 0$, $g'(x) \geq 0$ for $x \in \mathbb{R}$. $g'(x) = 0 \Rightarrow x = 0, y = k$

Therefore the graph of $y = g(x)$ has a point of inflexion at $(0, k)$ with zero gradient for $m = 0$.

(ii) State the range of values of m, the graph of $y = g(x)$ has one local maximum point and one local minimum point, and the coordinates of the local maximum and minimum. [2]

$g'(x) = 12x^2 - 2mx = 2x(6x - m) = 0 \Rightarrow x = 0, x = \dfrac{m}{6}$

$x = 0 \Rightarrow y = k$

$x = \dfrac{m}{6} \Rightarrow y = 4x^3 - mx^2 + k = \dfrac{108k - m^3}{108}$

The two stationary points are $(0, k)$ and $\left(\dfrac{m}{6}, \dfrac{108k - m^3}{108}\right)$.

If $m < 0$, the local maximum point is $\left(\dfrac{m}{6}, \dfrac{108k - m^3}{108}\right)$ and the local minimum point is $(0, k)$.

If $m > 0$, the local minimum point is $\left(\dfrac{m}{6}, \dfrac{108k - m^3}{108}\right)$ and the local maximum point is $(0, k)$.

10   [Maximum mark: 10]

The velocity of a particle, v m s^{-1}, at time t seconds is given by $v = 0.3t^2 - 2.4t + 3.6$. The graph of v against t, for $0 \leq t \leq 8$, is shown below.

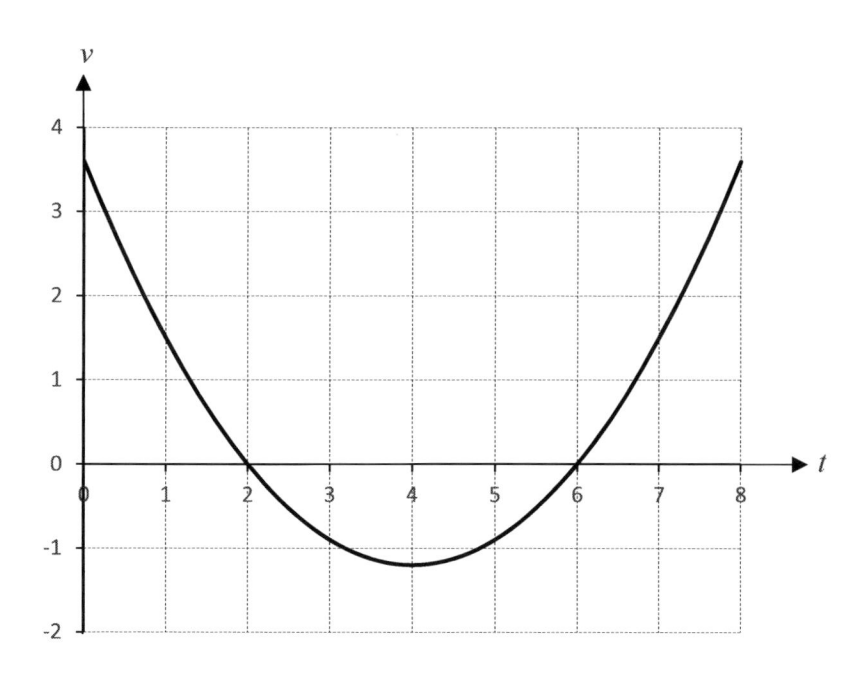

(a) Find the times when the particle stops. [2]

$t = 2, 6$

(b) Find the time when the particle move to the left. [2]

$2 < t < 6$

(c) Find the times when the particle move to the right. [2]

$0 \leq t < 2, 6 < t \leq 8$

(d) Find the time when the acceleration is 2.4 m s^{-2}. [1]

$\dfrac{dv}{dt} = 0.6t - 2.4$

$0.6t - 2.4 = 2.4 \Rightarrow t = 8$

(e) What is the displacement of the particle from the starting position when $t = 3$ seconds? [1]

$\displaystyle\int_0^3 (0.3t^2 - 2.4t + 3.6)\,dt = [0.1t^3 - 1.2t^2 + 3.6t]_0^3 = 2.7$ m

59

(f) Find the distance travelled by the particle in the first 3 seconds. [2]

$$\int_0^2 (0.3t^2 - 2.4t + 3.6)dt - \int_2^3 (0.3t^2 - 2.4t + 3.6)dt$$

$$= \int_0^2 (0.3t^2 - 2.4t + 3.6)dt - \int_0^3 (0.3t^2 - 2.4t + 3.6)dt$$

$$+ \int_0^2 (0.3t^2 - 2.4t + 3.6)dt$$

$$= 2\int_0^2 (0.3t^2 - 2.4t + 3.6)dt - \int_0^3 (0.3t^2 - 2.4t + 3.6)dt$$

$$= 2[0.1t^3 - 1.2t^2 + 3.6t]_0^2 - [0.1t^3 - 1.2t^2 + 3.6t]_0^3 = 3.7 \text{ m}$$

60

Paper 3 solutions

Section A – Short questions

1 [Maximum mark: 6]

PQRS is a trapezium, as shown in the diagram. $\widehat{SPQ} = 60°$. RQ is perpendicular to SR and PQ.

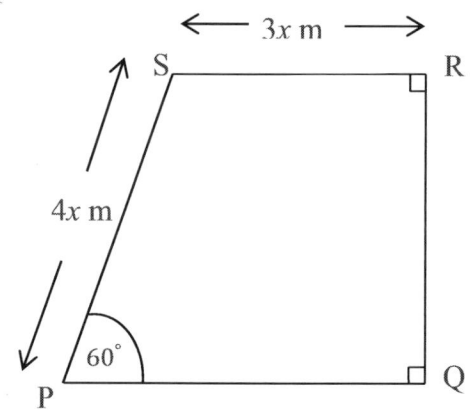

Diagram **NOT** accurately drawn

Work out the area of the trapezium, in terms of x.

The area of the trapezium is

$$\frac{(SR + PQ) \times SP \times \sin 60°}{2} = \frac{(SR + SR + SP \times \cos 60°) \times SP \times \sin 60°}{2}$$

$$= \frac{(3x + 3x + 4x \times \frac{1}{2}) \times 4x \times \frac{\sqrt{3}}{2}}{2} = 8\sqrt{3}x^2$$

2 [Maximum mark: 6]

The shape consists of two overlapping circles below. C₁ and C₂ are centres of the circles.

Find the perimeter of this shape.

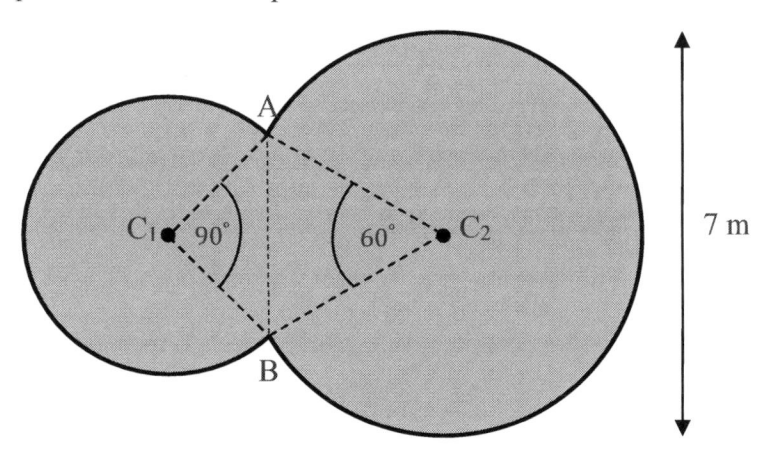

Give your answer in terms of π.

ABC₂ is an equilateral triangle.

$AB = AC_2 = \frac{7}{2}, AC_1 = AB \times \sin 45° = \frac{7}{2} \times \frac{\sqrt{2}}{2} = \frac{7\sqrt{2}}{4}$

The perimeter of this shape can be calculated as follows.

$\left(1 - \frac{90°}{360°}\right) \times \pi \times 2AC_1 + \left(1 - \frac{60°}{360°}\right) \times \pi \times 2AC_2 = \frac{3}{4} \times \pi \times \frac{7\sqrt{2}}{2} + \frac{5}{6} \times \pi \times 7$

$= \left(\frac{21\sqrt{2}}{8} + \frac{35}{6}\right) \pi \text{ m}$

3 [Maximum mark: 6]

(a) Show that $\log_4(\cos 2x + 2) = \log_2 \sqrt{\cos 2x + 2}$. [3]

$\log_4(\cos 2x + 2) = \frac{\log_2(\cos 2x + 2)}{\log_2 4} = \frac{\log_2(\cos 2x + 2)}{2} = \log_2 \sqrt{\cos 2x + 2}$

Therefore $\log_4(\cos 2x + 2) = \log_2 \sqrt{\cos 2x + 2}$

(b) Hence or otherwise solve $\log_2(2 \cos x) = \log_4(\cos 2x + 2)$ for $0 < x < \pi$. [3]

As $\log_4(\cos 2x + 2) = \log_2 \sqrt{\cos 2x + 2}$, we have

$\log_2(2 \cos x) = \log_2 \sqrt{\cos 2x + 2} \Rightarrow 4\cos^2(x) = \cos 2x + 2 \Rightarrow 4\cos^2(x)$

$= 2\cos^2(x) - 1 + 2 \Rightarrow \cos x = \pm \frac{\sqrt{2}}{2}$

As $0 < x < \pi$ and $\cos x > 0$, we have:

$x = \frac{\pi}{4}$

4 [Maximum mark: 6]

Two unbiased tetrahedral (four-sided) dice with faces labelled 1, 2, 3, 4 are thrown and the scores recorded. Let the random variables T be the minimum of these two scores. The probability distribution of T is given in the following table.

t	1	2	3	4
$P(T = t)$	$\frac{7}{16}$	a	b	$\frac{1}{16}$

(a) Find the value of a and the value of b. [4]

The following table can be obtained.

	1	2	3	4	← first die score
1	1	1	1	1	
2	1	2	2	2	
3	1	2	3	3	
4	1	2	3	4	

↑ second die score ↑ minimum of the two scores

From the table above, $a = \dfrac{5}{16}$ and $b = \dfrac{3}{16}$.

(b) Find the expected value of T. [2]

$$E(T) = 1 \times \frac{7}{16} + 2 \times \frac{5}{16} + 3 \times \frac{3}{16} + 4 \times \frac{1}{16} = \frac{15}{8}$$

5 [Maximum mark: 6]

A given polynomial function is defined as $f(x) = a_0 + a_1 x + a_2 x^2 + \cdots + a_n x^n$.

The roots of the polynomial equation $f(x) = 0$ are consecutive terms of a geometric sequence with a common ratio of 0.5 and first term 2.

Given that $a_{n-1} = -15$ and $a_n = 4$ find

(a) the degree of the polynomial; [3]

$$x_1 + x_2 + \cdots + x_n = -\frac{a_{n-1}}{a_n} = -\frac{-15}{4} = \frac{15}{4}$$

$$x_1 + x_2 + \cdots + x_n = \frac{2(1 - 0.5^n)}{1 - 0.5}$$

$$\frac{15}{4} = \frac{2(1 - 0.5^n)}{1 - 0.5} \Rightarrow 0.5^n = \frac{1}{16} \Rightarrow n = 4$$

The degree of the polynomial is 4.

(b) the value of a_0. [3]

$$x_1 x_2 x_3 x_4 = a \times ar \times ar^2 \times ar^3 = a^4 r^6$$

$$x_1 x_2 x_3 x_4 = (-1)^4 \frac{a_0}{a_4}$$

$$\Rightarrow a^4 r^6 = (-1)^4 \frac{a_0}{a_4} \Rightarrow a_0 = a_4 a^4 r^6 = 4 \times 2^4 0.5^6 = 1$$

The value of a_0 is 1.

6   [Maximum mark: 4]

(a)   Find $\int \cos^2(x)\,dx$ [2]

$$\int \cos^2(x)\,dx = \int \frac{\cos(2x)+1}{2}\,dx = \int \frac{2\cos(2x)}{4}\,dx + \int \frac{1}{2}\,dx = \frac{\sin(2x)}{4} + \frac{x}{2} + C$$

(b)   Hence, evaluate   [2]

$$\int_0^{\frac{\pi}{4}} \cos^2(x)\,dx = \left[\frac{\sin(2x)}{4} + \frac{x}{2}\right]_0^{\frac{\pi}{4}} = \left[\frac{\sin(2x)}{4}\right]_0^{\frac{\pi}{4}} + \left[\frac{x}{2}\right]_0^{\frac{\pi}{4}} = \frac{1}{4} + \frac{\pi}{8}$$

7   [Maximum mark: 6]

A set of 10 student group has a mean mass of 70 kg. A new student called Steve joins this group. The new mean mass of the 11 students is now 72 kg.

(a)   Find Steve's mass.   [3]

$\frac{\sum x}{10} = 70 \Rightarrow$

$\sum x = 700.$

Let Steve's mass be s.

$\frac{\sum x + s}{11} = 72 \Rightarrow$

$s = 11 \times 72 - \sum x = 11 \times 72 - 700 = 92$ kg

(b)   The new lower quartile and upper quartile for the masses of the 11 students are 66 kg and 76 kg respectively. Determine whether Steve's mass is an outlier, and justify your answer.   [3]

IQR $= 76 - 66 = 10$

$76 + 1.5 \times$ IQR $= 76 + 1.5 \times 10 = 91$

So Steve's mass of 92 kg is greater than $1.5 \times$ IQR above the upper quartile, Steve's mass is an outlier.

Section B – Long questions

8   [Maximum mark: 12]

(a)   On a single diagram, sketch the curve $y = 8x - x^2$ and the line $y = ax$, where $0 < a < 8$. [4]

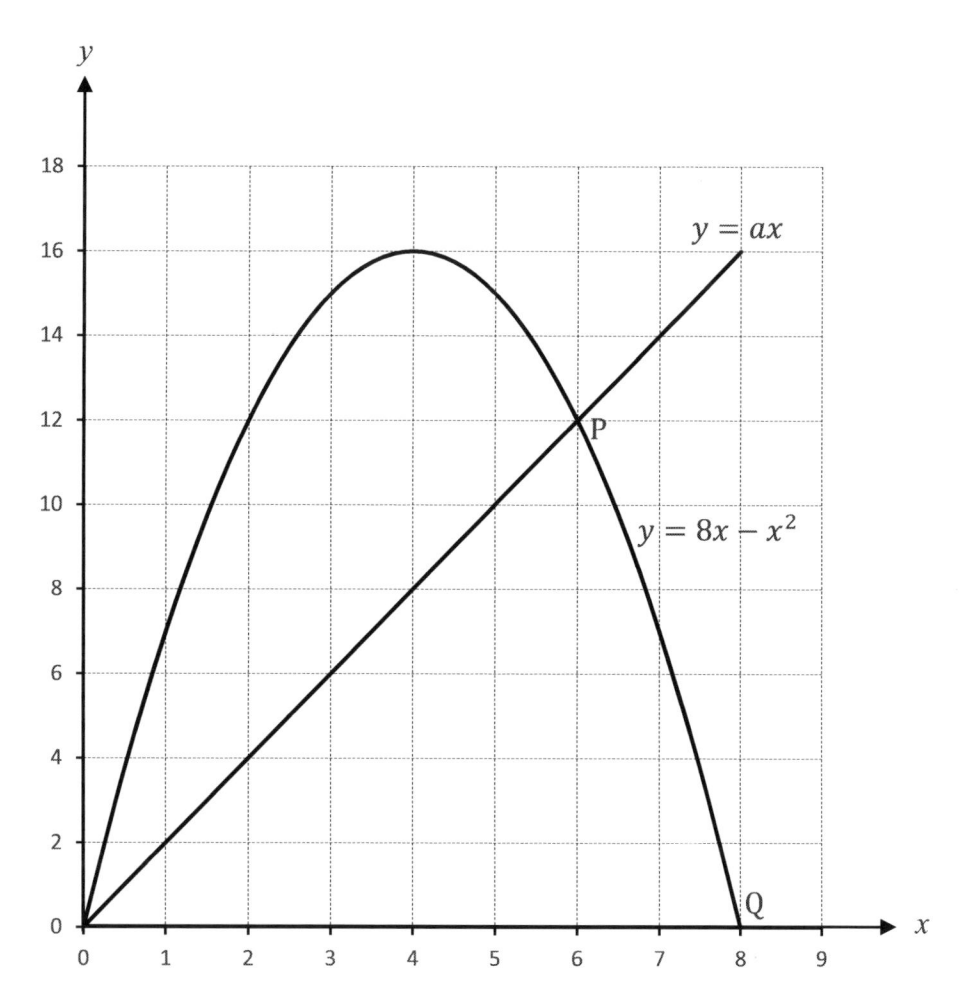

(b)   (i)   Show that the area of the finite region enclosed between the curve and the line is $\dfrac{(8-a)^3}{6}$. [4]

The line $y = ax$ intersects the curve at point P. The x-coordinate of point P can be calculated as follows:

$ax = 8x - x^2 \Rightarrow x(x + a - 8) = 0$

Therefore the x-coordinate of point P is $8 - a$

65

The area of the finite region enclosed between the curve and the line can be calculated as follows:

$$\int_0^{8-a} ((8x - x^2) - ax)dx = \int_0^{8-a} ((8-a)x - x^2)dx = \left[\frac{8-a}{2}x^2 - \frac{x^3}{3}\right]_0^{8-a}$$

$$= \frac{(8-a)^3}{2} - \frac{(8-a)^3}{3} = \frac{(8-a)^3}{6}$$

(ii) Given that this area is exactly one-eighth the area enclosed between the curve and the x-axis, determine the exact value of a. [4]

The x-axis intersects the curve at point $Q(8, 0)$.

The area enclosed between the curve and the x-axis is:

$$\int_0^8 (8x - x^2)dx = \left[4x^2 - \frac{x^3}{3}\right]_0^8 = \left[\frac{x^2(12-x)}{3}\right]_0^8 = \frac{64 \times 4}{3}$$

$$\frac{8 \times (8-a)^3}{6} = \frac{64 \times 4}{3} \Rightarrow (8-a)^3 = 64 \Rightarrow 8 - a = 4 \Rightarrow a = 4,$$

as $0 < a < 8$.

9   [Maximum mark: 15]

The heights in metres of a random sample of 80 cows in a field were measured and the following cumulative frequency graph obtained.

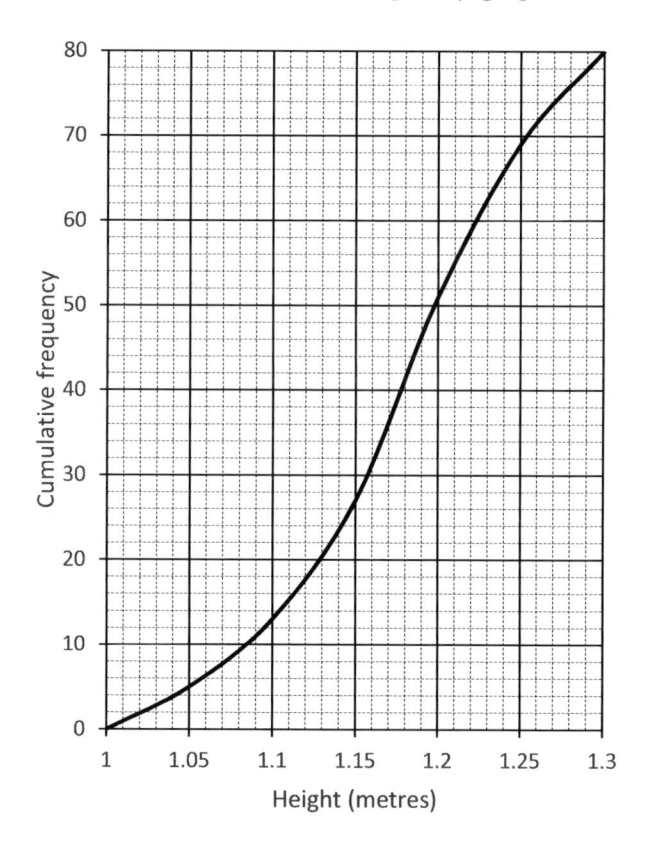

(a) Estimate the median of these data. [2]

Median position: 40th cow. 1.18 m

(b) Estimate the interquartile range for these data. [3]

Lower quartile position: 20th cow; Lower quartile: 1.13 m.

Upper quartile position: 60th cow; Upper quartile: 1.22 m.

Interquartile range: $1.22 - 1.13 = 0.09$ m.

(c) Draw a box-and-whisker diagram to summarize information of these data. [3]

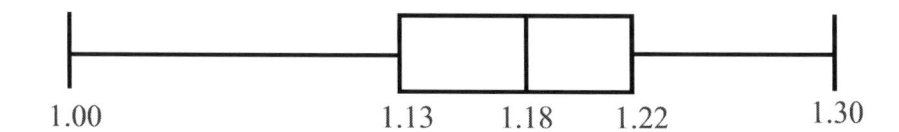

(d) Draw a frequency table for the heights of the cows, using a class width of 0.05 metres. [3]

Height (h metres)	Frequency
$1.00 < h \leq 1.05$	5
$1.05 < h \leq 1.10$	8
$1.10 < h \leq 1.15$	14
$1.15 < h \leq 1.20$	24
$1.20 < h \leq 1.25$	18
$1.25 < h \leq 1.30$	11

(e) A cow is selected at random.

(i) Find the probability that its height is less than or equal to 1.15 metres. [2]

There are 27 cows which the height is less than or equal to 1.15 metres.

The probability is:

$$P(h \leq 1.15) = \frac{27}{80}$$

(ii) Given that its height is less than or equal to 1.15 metres, find the probability that its height is less than or equal to 1.12 metres. [2]

There are 18 cows which the height is less than or equal to 1.12 metres, therefore

$$P(h \leq 1.12) = \frac{18}{80}$$

Given that its height is less than or equal to 1.15 metres, the probability that its height is less than or equal to 1.12 metres is:

$$P(h \leq 1.12 | h \leq 1.15) = \frac{P(h \leq 1.12)}{P(h \leq 1.15)} = \frac{\frac{18}{80}}{\frac{27}{80}} = \frac{2}{3}$$

10 [Maximum mark: 13]

Let $f(x) = x^3 - 6x^2 + 9x + 4$

(a) Find $f'(x)$. [2]

$f'(x) = 3x^2 - 12x + 9$

(b) Sketch the graph of $y = f'(x)$, indicating clearly the coordinates of minimum point, the x-axis intercepts, and the y-axis intercept. [3]

$f'(x) = 3x^2 - 12x + 9 = 3(x-2)^2 - 3 = 3(x-1)(x-3)$

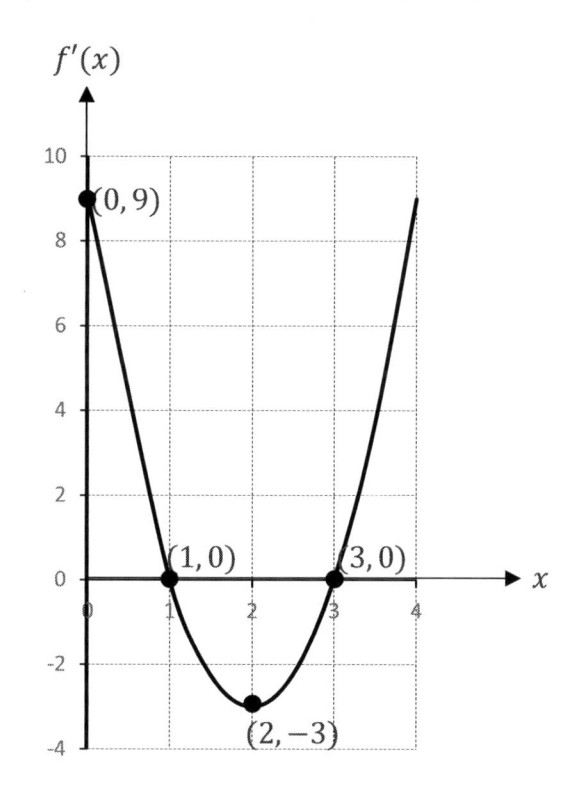

(c) Find all values of x for which $f(x)$ is increasing. [2]

For $x < 1$ and $x > 3$, $f'(x) > 0$, so that $f(x)$ is increasing for $x < 1$ and $x > 3$.

(d) Find $f''(x)$. [2]

$f''(x) = 6x - 12$

(e) Hence find and classify the stationary points on the graph of $y = f(x)$. [2]

When $x = 1, y = 8, f''(1) = -6$ so maximum.

When $x = 3, y = 4, f''(3) = 6$ so minimum.

(f) The equation $f(x) = k$ has three solutions. Find the possible values of k. [2]

When the equation $f(x) = k$ has three solutions, the k must be between the local maximum and minimum of $f(x) = x^3 - 6x^2 + 9x + 4$, so that $4 < k < 8$.

Paper 4 solutions

Section A – Short questions

1 [Maximum mark: 6]

A tunnel entrance has centre C and a circular arc of diameter 20 metres. The height of the tunnel entrance is 16 metres.

Work out the width of road surface (*w*) of the tunnel.

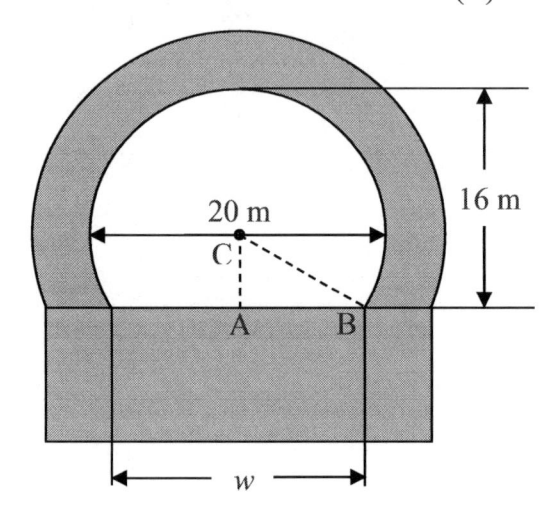

Draw a right-angled triangle ABC, as shown on the diagram. A is the midpoint of road surface of the tunnel.

$$AB = \sqrt{BC^2 - AC^2} = \sqrt{\left(\frac{20}{2}\right)^2 - (16-10)^2} = 8$$

$w = 2 \times AB = 2 \times 8 = 16 \text{ m}$

2   [Maximum mark: 6]

Here are a sphere and a cone. The base of the cone and the sphere have the same radius r cm. l, the slant height, is $\sqrt{17}r$ cm.

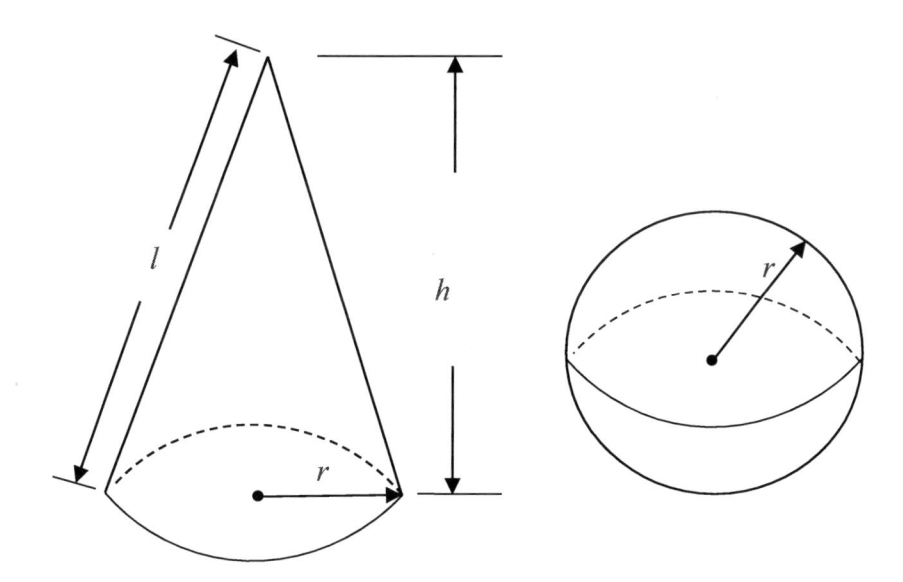

Prove that the sphere and the cone have the same volume.

h is the height of the cone.

$h = \sqrt{l^2 - r^2} = \sqrt{17r^2 - r^2} = 4r$

The volume of the sphere is

$\frac{4}{3}\pi r^3$

The volume of the cone is $\frac{1}{3}\pi r^2 h = \frac{1}{3}\pi r^2 \times 4r = \frac{4}{3}\pi r^3$

$\frac{1}{3}\pi r^2 h = \frac{1}{3}\pi r^2 \times 4r = \frac{4}{3}\pi r^3$

∴ The sphere and the cone have the same volume.

3   [Maximum mark: 5]

Solve $|2x + 1| = x^2 - 2$, where $x \in \mathbb{R}$.

For $x \geq -\dfrac{1}{2}$, $2x + 1 = x^2 - 2 \Rightarrow x^2 - 2x - 3 = 0 \Rightarrow (x - 3)(x + 1) = 0$

$\Rightarrow x = -1, 3$

Only $x = 3$ is the solution.

For $x < -\dfrac{1}{2}$, $2x + 1 = -x^2 + 2 \Rightarrow x^2 + 2x - 1 = 0 \Rightarrow x = -1 \pm \sqrt{2}$

Only $x = -1 - \sqrt{2}$ is the solution.

Therefore the solutions are $x = 3$ and $x = -1 - \sqrt{2}$.

4   [Maximum mark: 6]

A bag contains three counters numbered 1, 2 and 3 respectively. John selects one of these counters at random and he notes the number on the selected counter. He then tosses that number of fair coins.

(a) Calculate the probability that no head is obtained. [3]

P(no heads from n coins tossed) $= 0.5^n$

$P(\text{no head}) = \dfrac{1}{3} \times \dfrac{1}{2} + \dfrac{1}{3} \times \dfrac{1}{4} + \dfrac{1}{3} \times \dfrac{1}{8} = \dfrac{7}{24}$

(b) Given that no head is obtained, find the probability that he tossed two coins. [3]

$P(2 \text{ coins}|\text{no heads}) = \dfrac{P(2 \text{ coins and no heads})}{P(\text{no heads})} = \dfrac{\frac{1}{3} \times \frac{1}{4}}{\frac{7}{24}} = \dfrac{2}{7}$

5   [Maximum mark: 5]

In the expansion of $(x + 1)(x + p)^6$, where $p \in \mathbb{R}$, the coefficient of the term in x^5 is 21.

Find the possible values of p.

$(x + 1)(x + p)^6 = (x + 1)(\,^6C_0 x^6 p^0 + \,^6C_1 x^5 p^1 + \,^6C_2 x^4 p^2 + \cdots)$

The coefficient of the term in x^5 can be calculated as follows.

$^6C_1 p^1 + \,^6C_2 p^2 = 6p + 15p^2$

So $6p + 15p^2 = 21 \Rightarrow 5p^2 + 2p - 7 = 0 \Rightarrow (5p + 7)(p - 1) = 0 \Rightarrow p = -\dfrac{7}{5}, 1$

6	[Maximum mark: 6]

Give that $\int_{-3}^{3} f(x)dx = 12$ and $\int_{0}^{3} f(x)dx = 15$, find

(a)	$\int_{-3}^{0} (f(x) + 3)dx$ [3]

$$\int_{-3}^{0} (f(x)+3)dx = \int_{-3}^{0} f(x)dx + \int_{-3}^{0} 3dx = \int_{-3}^{3} f(x)dx - \int_{0}^{3} f(x)dx + \int_{-3}^{0} 3dx$$

$$= 12 - 15 + [3x]_{-3}^{0} = -3 + 9 = 6$$

(b)	$\int_{-3}^{0} f(x+3)dx$ [3]

Let $u = x + 3$, then $du = dx$

$$\int_{-3}^{0} f(x+3)dx = \int_{0}^{3} f(u)du = 15$$

7	[Maximum mark: 6]

A cylinder of radius r is inscribed in a sphere with centre O and radius R as shown in the following diagram. The height of the cylinder is h, X denotes the centre of its base and B a point where the cylinder touches the sphere.

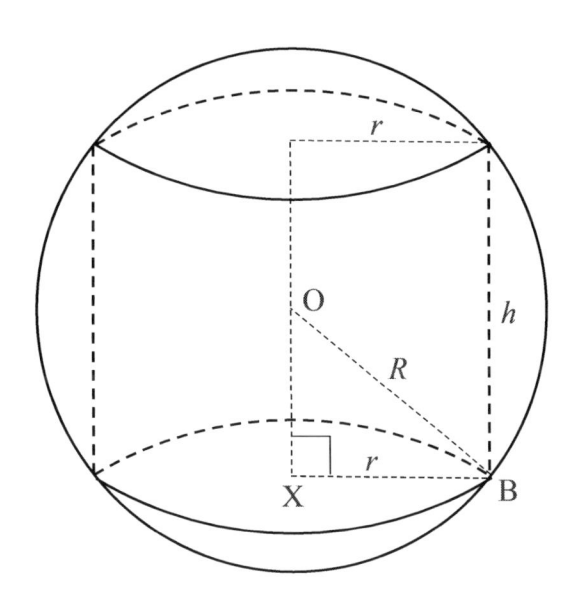

(a)	Show that the volume of the cylinder may be expressed by $V = \frac{\pi}{4}(4R^2h - h^3)$. [3]

$r^2 = R^2 - \left(\frac{h}{2}\right)^2$

$V = \pi r^2 h = \pi\left(R^2 - \left(\frac{h}{2}\right)^2\right)h = \frac{\pi}{4}(4R^2h - h^3)$

73

(b) Given that there is one inscribed cylinder having a maximum volume, show that the volume of this cylinder is $\frac{4\sqrt{3}\pi R^3}{9}$. [3]

$$\frac{dV}{dh} = \frac{\pi}{4}(4R^2 - 3h^2) = 0 \Rightarrow h = \sqrt{\frac{4}{3}}R$$

$$V = \frac{\pi}{4}(4R^2 h - h^3) = \frac{\pi}{4}\left(4R^2 \times \sqrt{\frac{4}{3}}R - \left(\sqrt{\frac{4}{3}}R\right)^3\right) = \frac{4\sqrt{3}\pi R^3}{9}$$

Section B – Long questions

8 [Maximum mark: 8]

(a) Sketch the graph of $f(x) = \dfrac{x+3}{2x+1}$, stating equations of any asymptotes and the coordinates of any points of intersection with the axes. [4]

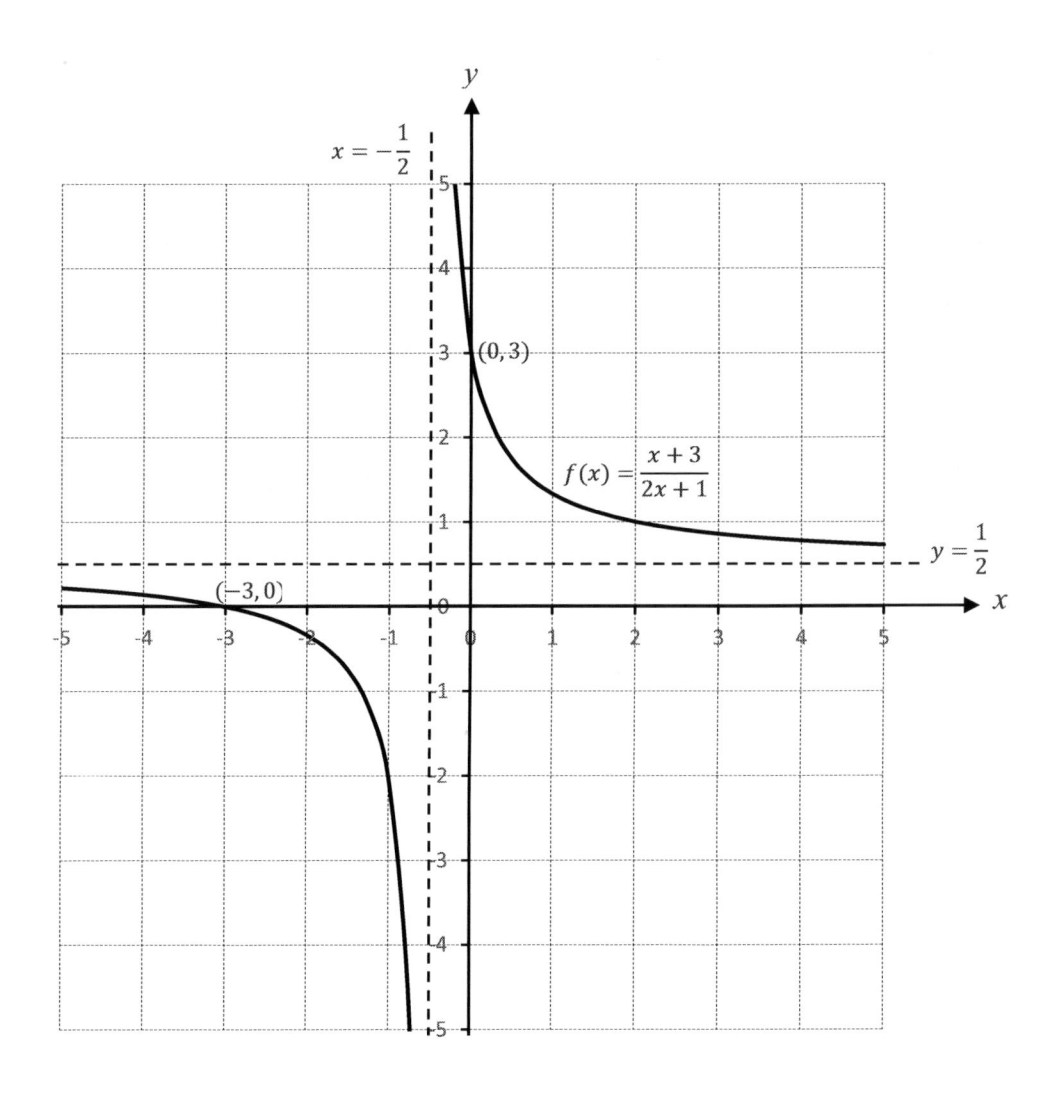

Asymptotes:

$x = -\frac{1}{2}; y = \frac{1}{2}$

Vertical asymptote:

$\lim_{x \to -\frac{1}{2}^-} f(x) = -\infty; \quad \lim_{x \to -\frac{1}{2}^+} f(x) = \infty$

Horizontal asymptote:

$\lim_{x \to \infty} f(x) = \frac{1}{2}$

(b) Consider the function $g: x \to \sqrt{\dfrac{x+3}{2x+1}}$

Write down

(j) the largest possible domain of g; [2]

$\dfrac{x+3}{2x+1} \geq 0 \Rightarrow x > -\dfrac{1}{2}; x \leq -3$

(ii) the corresponding range of g. [2]

$g(x) \geq 0;$

$g(x) \neq \dfrac{1}{\sqrt{2}} \Rightarrow g(x) \neq \dfrac{\sqrt{2}}{2}$

9   [Maximum mark: 15]

200 vehicles are tested for their air pollution efficiency. The results are given in the cumulative frequency graph.

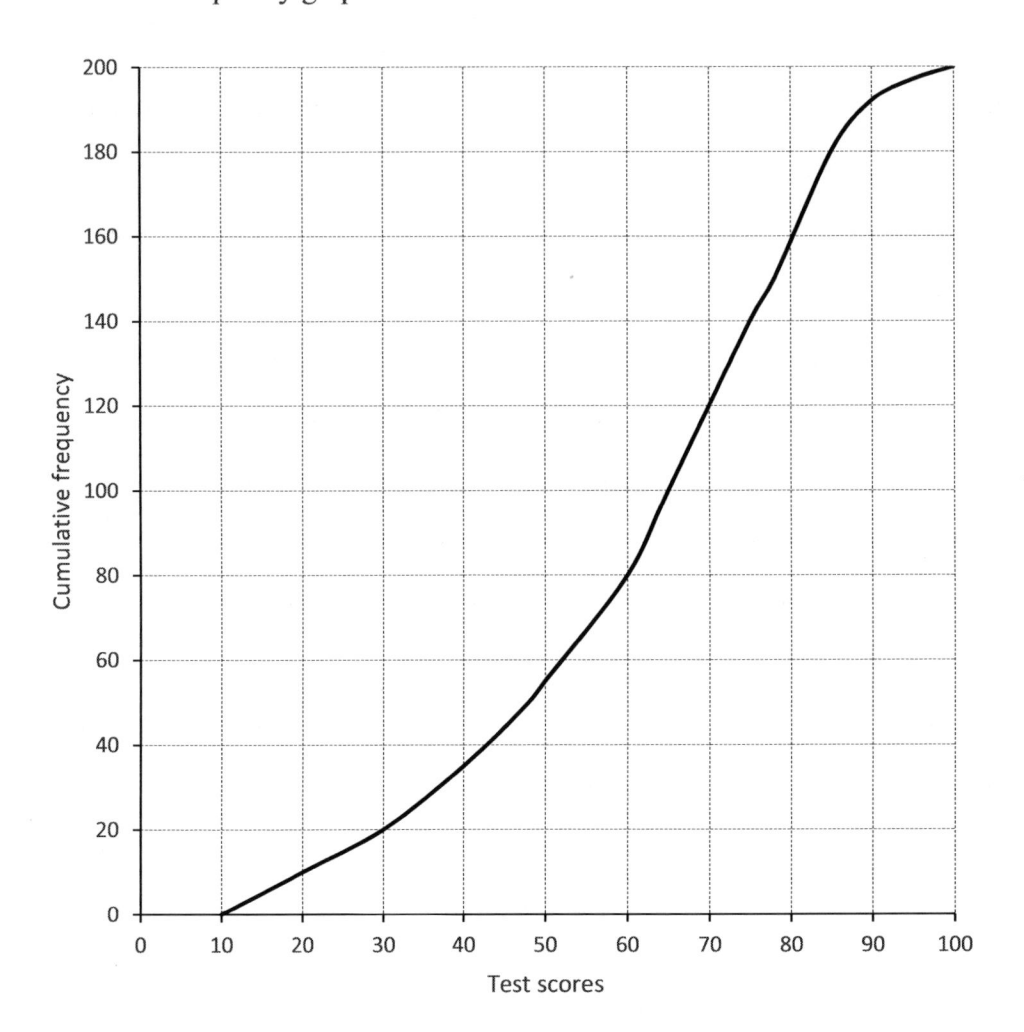

(a)   Estimate the median test score. [2]

Median position: 100th vehicle. The median score: 65.

(b)   Estimate the interquartile range for this data. [3]

Lower quartile position: 50th vehicle; Lower quartile: 48.

Upper quartile position: 150th vehicle; Upper quartile: 78.

Interquartile range: $78 - 48 = 30$.

(c) The top 10% of the vehicles receive a lower insurance premium price A and the next best 20% of the vehicles receive a price B. Estimate

(i) the minimum score required to obtain a price A; [2]

The top 20 vehicles receive a lower insurance premium price A, the estimate minimum score is 85, by using the 180th vehicle.

(ii) the minimum score required to obtain a price B. [2]

The next best 20% of the vehicles receive a price B, the estimate minimum score is 75, by using the 140th vehicle.

(d) A vehicle is selected at random.

(i) Find the probability that its score is less than or equal to 85. [2]

There are 180 vehicles which the score is less than or equal to 85.

The probability is:

$$P(s \leq 85) = \frac{180}{200}$$

(ii) Given that its score is less than or equal to 85, find the probability that it has a price B. [4]

There are 20% vehicles which receive a price B

$$P(75 \leq s < 85) = \frac{40}{200}$$

Given that its score is less than or equal to 85, find the probability that it has a price B.

$$P(75 \leq s < 85 | s \leq 85) = \frac{P(75 \leq s < 85)}{P(s \leq 85)} = \frac{\frac{40}{200}}{\frac{180}{200}} = \frac{2}{9}$$

10 [Maximum mark: 17]

Given that $f(x) = 3xe^{-x}$ for $-3 \leq x \leq 3$

(a) Show that $f(x)$ has one turning point and one point of inflection. [4]

$f(x) = 3xe^{-x} \Rightarrow f'(x) = 3e^{-x} - 3xe^{-x} = 3e^{-x}(1-x)$

$\Rightarrow f''(x) = -3e^{-x} - 3e^{-x} + 3xe^{-x} = 3e^{-x}(x-2)$

Turning point at $f'(x) = 0 \Rightarrow 3e^{-x}(1-x) \Rightarrow x = 1$

Inflection point at $f''(x) = 0 \Rightarrow 3e^{-x}(x-2) \Rightarrow x = 2$

x	$x < 2$	$x > 2$
Sign of f''	−	+
Concavity of f	down	up

Since $f''(2) = 0$ and the function changes concavity at $x = 2$, there is a point of inflection at $x = 2$.

(b) Identity the nature of the turning point and state its coordinates. [2]

$f(1) = 3e^{-1} = \dfrac{3}{e} \Rightarrow$ Turning point at $\left(1, \dfrac{3}{e}\right)$

$f''(1) = 3e^{-1}(1-2) < 0 \Rightarrow \left(1, \dfrac{3}{e}\right)$ is a maximum.

(c) Find the coordinates of the point of inflection and hence sketch the graph of $f(x)$. [4]

$f(2) = 6e^{-2} = \dfrac{6}{e^2} \Rightarrow$ point of inflection at $\left(2, \dfrac{6}{e^2}\right)$

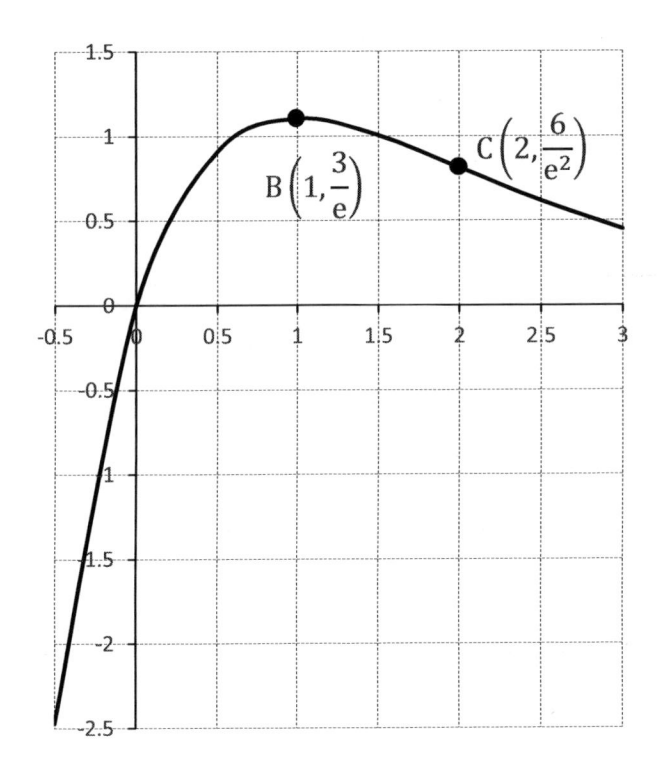

78

(d) Find the equation of the tangent to the curve at the point of inflection. [2]

Gradient of tangent at $x = 2$ is given by

$$f'(2) = 3e^{-2}(1-2) = -\frac{3}{e^2}$$

Therefore the equation of tangent can be obtained as follows

$$y - \frac{6}{e^2} = -\frac{3}{e^2}(x-2) \Rightarrow y = -\frac{3}{e^2}x + \frac{12}{e^2}$$

(e) Determine the coordinates of the tangent where this tangent meets the x-axis. [2]

$y = 0 \Rightarrow x = 4$

The coordinates are (4, 0).

(f) Calculate the area bounded by this tangent and the x- and y-axes. [3]

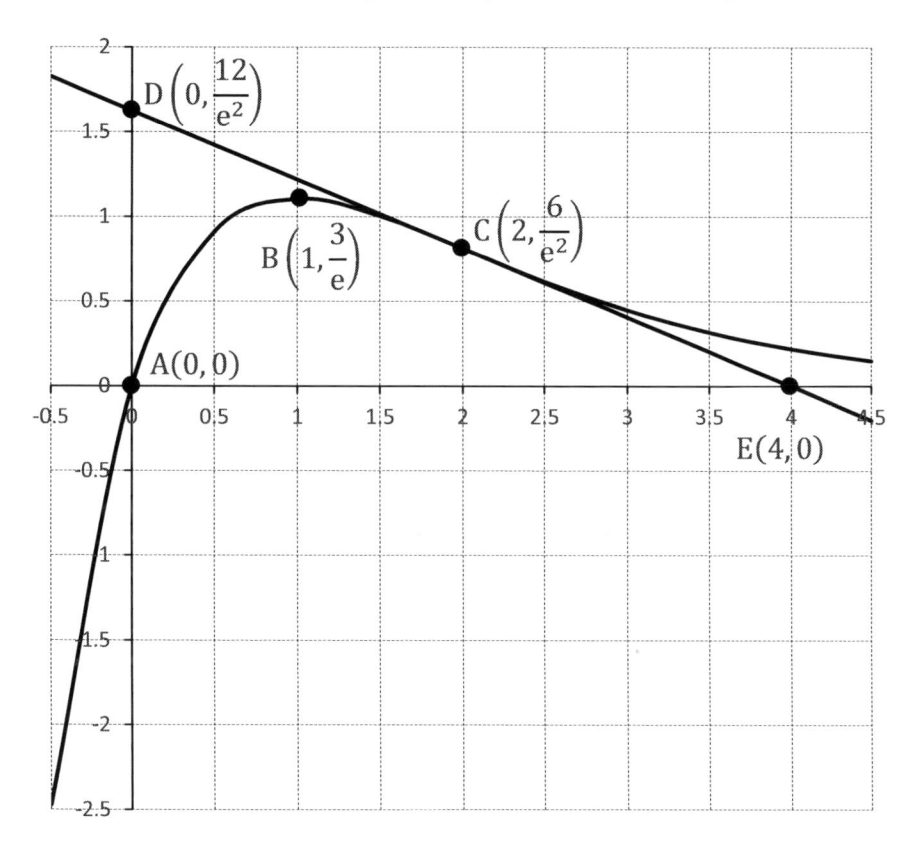

$x = 0 \Rightarrow y = \frac{12}{e^2}$

The area bounded by this tangent and the x- and y-axes can be calculated is the area of triangle ADE.

$$\frac{1}{2} \times 4 \times \frac{12}{e^2} = \frac{24}{e^2}$$

Printed in Great Britain
by Amazon